BBC Radio Mers Team

A GUIDED TO   SIDE
ITS WILDLIFE AND NATURAL HISTORY

Compiled by
Bob *'The Birdman'* Hughes

Published by:- Avid Publications,
Garth Boulevard
Bebington,
Wirral,
Merseyside. UK
CH63 5LS
Telephone / Fax: (44) 0151 645 2047
e-mail info@avidpublications.co.uk
website http//www.avidpublications.co.uk

BBC Radio Merseyside NATURE WATCH
Compiled by Bob Hughes

ISBN 1 902964 24 1 © BBC RADIO MERSEYSIDE 2002
A CIP record for this book is available from the British Library

**OTHER BOOKS AND VIDEOS AVAILBLE DIRECT FROM
AVID PUBLICATIONS ARE DETAILED AT THE REAR OF
THIS BOOK**

by *BILL ODDIE*

I was quite startled when I saw the contents of this book. It was the first time I had seen reports on the Grand National, The FA Cup Final, the Beatles, pop concerts and a 10K road race in a nature book!

But when I took a closer look I realized it was the perfect way to present a picture of the nature and wildlife of an urban area like Merseyside, where the dominant species is, well, 'us'.

Bob Hughes and the Nature Watch team are not eccentric isolates. Far from it, they are very much part of the local 'scene' and enjoy it along with everybody else. But on route through the Merseyside calendar they have kept their eyes open, noticing the things that so many people simply don't see: Goldfinches in the trees above your head; Mistle Thrushes nesting on the lamppost in the car park, beautiful marsh orchids in the corner of that piece of 'wasteland' where a whole colony of common blue butterflies flourishes - right in the city centre!

You certainly have a unique 'patch' here on Merseyside. To you it may sound perfectly normal to go nature watching to world famous locations such as Penny Lane, Strawberry Field, Anfield and Aintree... but to others it is simply mind-boggling. Then a Ferry 'Cross the Mersey to see Peregrines, yes Peregrines nesting up on the local railway station just across the river from the Pier Head.

I remember feeling these 'vibes' when I was on Merseyside myself, putting together the 'Bill Oddie Goes Wild' special about Liverpool and the Merseyside region, which was broadcast for BBC TV in January 2001.

So I am very happy to see that BBC Radio Merseyside continues to broadcast a weekly report of local nature news - the *real* news to the many people who still try to live in some sort of harmony with nature. As Bob himself always says: 'Happy Watching!'

List of Contributors

Kathy Andrews, Garston
Marian Arnould, Leasowe
Alan Astley, Oldham

Andy Bayley, Canning Place Fire Station
Brian Bradley, Maghull
Mrs M. Briscoe, Stoneycroft
Mrs E. Bone, Wavertree
Noel and Hazel Blundell, Neston
Andy Ball, BBC Radio Merseyside
Maurice Bray, Anglican Cathedral
Sheila Binks, Childwall
Ron Billingsley, Huyton
Steve Burke, Oxton and mum Vera
Richard Baker, Liverpool City Ranger
David Bryant, Merseyside Naturalists Assoc.

Tony Craven, Huyton
Eric Coates, Bebington
Sheila Colley, Thurstaston
Joyce Carter, Anfield
Joe Carter, Halewood
Janet Croker, Claire House
Val Curtis, Thingwall
Steve Capstick, BBC TV
Ted Cregeen, Aigburth
John Clegg, MNA, Kirkdale
Jeff Clarke, Wirral Rangers
Stephen Coathup, Neston
Les Coe, Williamson Tunnels
Don Charlton, Friends of Bidston Moss

Audrey Davies, Bebington
Ron Davies, BBC Radio Merseyside
Mike Dinsmore, New Brighton
Arthur Davies, Maritime Museum
Jan Davies, Bebington, Wirral
John Drew, Manor Trust, Poulton, Wallasey
Joe Ellis, Netherton
Ray Eades, Hull
Madeleine Evans, Garston News
Margaret Eastman, Port Sunlight

Eamon Farrell, Maritime Museum
Rodney Fletcher, Maghull

Brenda and Jim Fitzsimons, Bowring Park
Mr and Mrs S and I Freeman, New Brighton
Joan Fisher, Liscard, Wallasey
Neil Farrell, Sefton Park
Stephen Fletcher, Halewood
Greg Flynn, Liverpool 6
Andrew Fell, Inshore Rescue, Pier Head

Mick and Betty Griffiths, West Kirby
Vera Gordon, Crosby
Justin Garside - Taylor, Maritime Museum
Sid Gore, Maghull
Cath Gordon, Kirkdale
Jean and John Geddis, Widnes

David Holland, Gateacre
Muriel Hammond, Garston
Mary Humphreys, Liverpool 4
Mrs E.M. Harper, Queens Drive, Ullet Road
Val Holland, Calderstones
Mrs T. Helsby, Thornton Hough
Lenny Hoare, Liscard, Wallasey
Mrs G. Hughes, Wallasey
Derek Hampson, RSPCA, Liverpool
David Herring, Newsham Park
Margaret Higgins, Irby, Wirral
Pat Hughes, Litherland
Bob Hughes, Widnes (another one: not me!)
Shirley Hudson, Netherton
Mrs F. Heyes, Aintree

Malcolm Ingham, Thurstaston Country Park

Irene and Edmund Jelley, West Kirby
Ann and Alan Jones, Childwall
B. Johnson, Port Sunlight
John Jakeman, Bidston Hill
Mrs B. Jones, Burscough
Rosaline Jane, Upton, Wirral
Martyn Jamieson, Wirral Rangers
Ann Jeffries, Woolton
Bill Jones, Garston News
Alan Jones, Garston Under the Bridge

Joe and Margaret Kennedy, Anfield
Jackie Kenyon, St Edward s College

Ann Kelty, Maghull
Paul Kelly, Maritime Museum
Frank Kingsbury, Bowring Park
Earl Kirkham, Sefton Park
Alan Kennaugh, Friends of Bidston Moss

Gladys and Billy Lea, Netherley
Sue Landsborough, Upton, Wirral
Mrs Betty Lloyd, Hunts Cross
Mrs M. Lees, Liverpool 15
Miss Maisee Liversage, West Kirby
Peter Lyons, New Ferry
Adrian Leigh, Fazakerley

Kevin McNulty, Bootle
Alan McGlynn, Sefton Park
Miss M.Marr, New Brighton
Amy Melville, Fazakerley
E. McGlincy, Birkenhead
John McGowan, Hamilton Square Station
Linda McDermott, BBC Radio Merseyside
Gerry Marsden, Ferry Cross the Mersey
Ken and Val Mason, Allerton
Fiona and Chris Marsden, Stoneycroft
Wilf Murray, Aigburth
J.Nicholas, Speke
Mary and Peter Owen, Formby
Phil O Sullivan, St Helens

Margaret Parry, Stoneycroft
Dennis Price, Wallasey Village
Joan and Ian Pickavance, Irby
Veronica Powell, Cronton
Wendie Pitt, Chester
Jim Prendergast, Mersey Tunnels
Poulton Primary School, Wallasey
Peter Price, Royal Liver Building
Graham Paisley, St Peters, Woolton
Quiggins, Harry and the boys (and girls!)
        College Lane, city centre

Ken and Norma Richardson, Gateacre
L. Rowlands and family, Bebington
Pat and Peter Robinson, West Derby
Walter Roughsedge, Sefton Park
Mary Robinson, Saughall Massie
Kathleen Renton, Strawberry Field

Margaret Ratcliffe, Bootle
David Roberts, BBC Radio Merseyside
Gordon Roberts, Speke
Mrs Rushworth, Heswall

Ann Smart, Breck Road, Liverpool
Mrs C. Stewart, Heswall, Wirral
H. Shalliker, Maghull
Mrs L. Saunders, Wallasey
Roger Summerskill, BBC Radio Merseyside
Margaret and Gerry Sharpe, Childwall
Ivor Scholes, St Michaels Hamlet
Paul Sutter, Liverpool City Rangers
Adrienne Stratford, Caernarfon
Robin and Jake Surtees, Aigburth
Trevor Smith, Aintree
Paul Sutton, HM Coastguard
Mrs E. Swann, Southport

Margaret Thompson, Penny Lane
Mr and Mrs S.A. Thomas, Garston
Audrey Thomas, Hoylake
Heather Vaughan, West Derby
Shari Vahl, BBC Radio Merseyside

Tony Whewell, Crosby
Dorothy Wardley, Moreton
Thelma Westell, Ormskirk
Joanna Williams, RSPCA, Wallasey
Shaun Wilson, Woolton
Geoffrey Winstanley, Whiston
K.W. Williams, Liverpool University
Mrs J. Wade, Birkenhead
Glynn Williams, West Derby
Ruby Williams, BBC Radio Merseyside
Graham White, BBC Radio Merseyside
Goronwy Wynne, Fflint, North Wales
Annabelle Wynne-Jones, BBC Radio Merseyside
Father James Williams, St Anthonys, Scotland Road
Archie Weir, Friends of Bidston Moss

Julia Yeardsley, Bromborough

Apologies to those whose names may have inadvertently been omitted... but you all contributed to this book..it is yours... you wrote it.

A MESSAGE FROM THE LIVER BIRDS

We want to turn Merseyside into the biggest wildlife park, the biggest 'nature reserve' in the country! The streets, the gardens and the parks, the backyards and roof tops – there is just as much going on here in town as there is 'out there' in the country – and it deserves just as much attention.

Everybody can join in by watching their own 'patch' – even if that simply means your own backyard or garden, a walk with the dog, to the shops, to school, from the car to your work place. All sightings and observations – in both town *and* country – are worth recording – and reporting.

So we are inviting you to send in records of anything and everything you see, so that we can compile a picture of what's going on on Merseyside, week by week, through the seasons of the year. We've even included extra pages at the back of this book for you to make any notes on your observations.

Nature is painting for us, day by day, pictures of infinite

beauty, if only we have the eyes to see them.

John Ruskin (1819-1900)

Waxwings in Netherton Way, Bootle (by the Giro) – photo Martin Bridge

JANUARY

SIBERIAN WAXWINGS INVADE MERSEYSIDE:

The year got off to a great start with reports of Waxwings which had first been seen in Scotland around Christmas. They were now moving south and invading the rest of Britain, including Merseyside. The nearest place that Waxwings nest is somewhere out the back of Petersburg in Russia and it is only about once every ten years that a large invasion takes place on this scale, presumably when berries are in short supply in their homelands or when temperatures are exceedingly low (-35C in Siberia in Jan-Feb!).

Reports started coming in from all parts of Merseyside and I went down to see the flock which had discovered the rowan berries in Briardale Road, Seacombe, only a mile or so across the river from the Pier Head.

The casual passer-by could easily overlook them as a flock of Starlings when they sit on telephone wires or TV aerials, but they are unmistakable at close range with their pinkish-brown colouring and bushy heads of 'hair'. It was wonderful to see about thirty of these exotic birds all the way from Siberia down a back street of terraced houses in Seacombe on the rowan berries outside a small block of new flats. But the local Mistle Thrushes were not all pleased to see them: they had reserved these berries as their winter larder and tried to defend the trees, chasing the Waxwings back up onto telephone wires when they could, but they were simply overwhelmed by numbers.

When I went back in February the berries had all gone – and so, of course, the Waxwings, but reports kept coming in from other parts of Merseyside into March and even April. The last reports I heard were from Townsend Avenue.

In January and February Waxwings were around the Palm House in Sefton Park. When ice forms on the lakes foxes often go out onto the ice to retrieve duck and moorhens which have died and which are kept fresh by the ice – Reynard's larder!

Alan McGlynn

Swan Lake: Swan 7GB and partner at Bidston Dock pool Summer 2000

6 JANUARY: WILDFOWL WINTER AT MARTIN MERE...

The number of Whooper Swans from Iceland and Bewick Swans from Siberia spending the winter at the Wildfowl and Wetlands Trust reserve at Martin Mere had been rapidly increasing, no doubt largely as a result of the feeding programme they have there (£40,000 annual bill!). Over 1,400 Whoopers and a hundred Bewicks were reported in January. Icelandic Pinkfooted Geese had always been the attraction at Martin Mere (8,000 reported in January) and I remember going on an annual 'pilgrimage', crawling along ditches and dykes to get good views of the geese over 40 years ago, well before Sir Peter Scott created the reserve there that we know today.

13 JANUARY: ...AND AT SOUTHPORT MARINE LAKE:

A lot of Mute Swans, Canada Geese and various species of duck spend the winter at the lake in Southport, where they know they will be well fed by visitors and residents alike. I went there myself on a special mission – to see if I could find 'my' swans, the swans which had nested at the pool by Bidston Dock the previous summer, the male with a blue ring, number 7GB, born in Powys in 1997 who spent the previous winter in Southport.

I didn't find 'my' swans amongst the 70 or so swans at Southport that day and no reports since – until 4 December .

THE RIVER MERSEY: A WILDFOWL HAVEN OF INTERNATIONAL IMPORTANCE:

The majority of people living in the Merseyside region do not realise that the Mersey itself – right on our doorstep – is a winter home to thousands of ducks and waders which move down from breeding areas in the polar regions. The huge flocks of Pintail, Wigeon, Teal and other ducks are not often seen because access to the marshes and tidal mudflats between Stanlow Oil Refinery and Frodsham is difficult.

BBC RADIO MERSEYSIDE GARDEN BIRD WATCH

City centre bird feeding centre – Jackie Newby, Upper Pitt Street

HUNT'S CROSS: I have a Scots pine and fir trees, juniper and silver birch in my garden and Blue Tit, Great Tit, Coal Tit, Long Tailed Tits, Wren, Chaffinch, Blackbird, Robin, Magpie (ugh!), Crows, Woodpigeons – but no Starlings or Sparrows. Betty Lloyd

CALDERSTONES: I have lived in Calderstones for some 15 years. In our garden we have daily visits from Greenfinch, Goldfinch, Chaffinch, Blue Tit, Great Tit, Coal Tit, Long Tailed Tit, nesting Blackbirds, a Thrush, Starlings, Robins and this year Crows. However, like many others in the Merseyside area we do not have any Sparrows.   Val Holland

KIRKDALE: Birds seen in my garden: Magpies, Blackbird, (brown) Thrush, Blue Tits – no Sparrows   Mary Humphreys

FAZAKERLEY: I live in Fazakerley and I have sparrows, Blackbirds, thrushes, Blue Tits, Great Tits, Goldfinches, Robins, Starlings, doves, and Wrens. I love to sit and watch them all eating the food I leave out for them.   Amy Melville

NETHERLEY: The birds we have had coming down into our garden over the past 32 years have been mostly Starlings, sparrows, Blue Tits, Great Tits, Woodpigeons and Collared Doves. We have also had Chaffinch, Greenfinch and our regular Robin. We have had to our great surprise a pair of Goldfinches. Magpies and Crows and almost every day a Heron flies over. Over the years we have enjoyed our birds, it's great to watch them. As you might have gathered we are both a couple of recycled teenagers!   Gladys and Billy Lea

LISCARD, Wallasey: There are some lovely birds we have in our back garden. Well it isn't really a garden, more like a posh yard. Every day at 9 am, 1 pm and 5 pm we have a visit from two lovely coloured birds, I think they are Goldfinches. We also have Blue Tits, Sparrows, Blackbird, Thrush, even a Woodpigeon. I really enjoy sitting watching the antics of these lovely birds.   Joan Fisher

4

WOODCOCK FLIES INTO NEW BRIGHTON WINDOW: One afternoon in January this year a Woodcock flew into our neighbour's window. It was stunned and unconscious for about half an hour, then recovered and flew away eventually. We are curious to know where it might have come from. It was snowing and there was a SW gale that day.

Miss M. Marr

This Woodcock was obviously moving away from hard weather to the north. They are very shy but not as rare as many people think. Maurice Bray at the Anglican Cathedral tells me he often finds the remains of Woodcock on the cathedral roof – from Peregrine kills.

BEBINGTON: We have the following birds: Robins, Sparrows (about a dozen), Great Tit, Blue Tit, Blackbird, Woodpigeon, Collared Dove, Wrens, sometimes Jay and occasional Magpie. A Heron sometimes passes through: we have a pond...

Eric Coates

UPTON, Wirral: We spotted these birds in one hour: Greenfinch, Robin, Blue Tit, Great Tit, Coal Tit, Blackbird, Magpie, Sparrow, Woodpigeon, Collared Dove, Dunnock. This year we are missing our Wren and Mistle Thrush. No Starlings and a decline(!) in Magpies.. Occasional Long Tailed Tit . Sue Landsborough

WINTERING BLACKCAPS IN MERSEYSIDE GARDENS: A Blackcap was sharing the same trees as winter Redwings and Chaffinches on the Breck, Wallasey, where it spent the whole winter, turning up in various gardens and even coming out with some song on sunny days in February and March.

CHILDWALL: I am thrilled to have a pair of Blackcaps visit us daily from nearby Black Woods. The male is light in colour with a jet black cap whilst the female is similar but with a chestnut cap. Norma Richardson

GATEACRE: We've had a winter Blackcap for eight successive weeks now. We had two Goldfinches and a record number of 15 species in the last week of January, 13 on one day. David Holland

CHILDWALL: We've seen a female Blackcap (after fat), Robin, Dunnock, Blackbird, Thrush, Sparrowhawk, Blue Tit, Coal Tit, Woodpigeons, Magpies, Wren.

Gerard and Margaret Sharpe

RESULTS OF RSPB NATIONAL GARDEN BIRDWATCH 27-28 JANUARY

Over 60 species were recorded in gardens nationwide, including Waxwings, Lesser Spotted Woodpecker and Kingfisher. 50,000 people took part in the weekend survey. Merseyside's Top Ten (with average number of birds per garden): Starling (4.0); Blackbird (3.3 – what does 0.3 of a Blackbird look like?!); House Sparrow (2.9); Blue Tit (2.9); Robin (1.4); Greenfinch (1.3); Chaffinch (1.3); Collared Dove (1.3); Woodpigeon (1.2); Great Tit (1.2). House Sparrows moved down one place compared with January 2000.

FEBRUARY: EARLY SIGNS OF SPRING ON MERSEYSIDE:

1 FEBRUARY: First Coltsfoot in flower. Magpies had been working on nests since the New Year and a pair of foxes had been seen out frolicking in the sunshine on 24 January. Mistle Thrushes were already building nests and Long Tailed Tits would soon be starting.

8 FEBRUARY: First Snowdrops and Forsythia in flower in a garden on the 'sunny side of the street'.

9 FEBRUARY: Song Thrush singing at 5.30, well before dawn. Many people reported 'green flares' in the sky – as we passed through an asteroid belt (called Alpha Aurigids - or something like that!).

11 FEBRUARY: "And the sweet silver song of a lark"... First Skylarks were singing over Bidston Moss, less than 3 miles from the Pier Head.

13 FEBRUARY: More Snowdrops and Daffodils. In a mild sunny spell around midday, just as I was thinking: "now if I was a butterfly...."- a Small Tortoiseshell flew through the garden, tempted out of hibernation early by the seductive warmth of midday.

IRBY, Wirral: Regular garden visitors include two pairs of Blackbirds, Sparrows, Collared Doves, Woodpigeons, Thrush, Blue Tit, Great Tit, Coal Tit, Jay, Robin, Sparrowhawk. Rarer visitors: Long Tailed Tit, Great Spotted Woodpecker, Siskin (last winter), Bullfinch. I walk in Royden Woods each day and regularly see Green Woodpeckers, Robins, Jays, Blackbirds and Tits, also Tree Creeper. We often see foxes and have toads, newts and frogs in the garden, field mice and possibly one dormouse.   Joan and Ian Pickavance

QUEENS DRIVE, LIVERPOOL 4: In my back garden I see 10-12 Sparrows, a thrush (sometimes two), Blackbird and at least four Great Tits. They are all regular visitors daily. I do my best to help the wildlife: it is so sad they are becoming so scarce.   Joyce Carter

CRONTON: Goldfinch, Greenfinch, Chaffinch, Robin Wren, sparrow, Blackbird, Mistle Thrush, Jay, Collared Dove, Woodpigeon, Magpie, Heron, Blue Tit, Coal Tit, Great Tit. We also have a nearly all white Blackbird which I call 'Whitey'. He's beautiful!

Veronica Powell

MAGHULL: Blackbirds, Wren, Tits of all types. Greenfinch, Chaffinch, Collared Dove, Woodpigeons, Sparrows and Starlings – and those ordinary pigeons and the 'blasted' Magpie. Also a visiting Heron – frustrated because my ponds are covered with wire etc!

H. Shalliker

Canning Dock early morning

The Alders in Chavasse Park

7

Gull Roost, Kings Dock. Woodside in background.

Cormorant in Brunswick Dock

16 FEB: PIER HEAD TO PARADISE (STREET) CITY NATURE TRAIL
VIA ALBERT DOCK AND CHAVASSE PARK

FIRST NATURE WATCH BROADCAST ON 'MORNING MERSEYSIDE': I was able to give an update of what had been going on so far since the beginning of the year and then at 7.00 I went out to explore the local surroundings to see what I could find. The plan was to walk a regular route through this nationally – and internationally – famous part of the city to see what turned up during the course of the year. It was quite unique, of course, to be able to include the Liver Birds up on the Liver Buildings, the Pier Head and Ferry Cross the Mersey in our city centre nature trail, not to mention the Albert Dock, the Merseyside Maritime Museum, the Museum of Liverpool Life, the Tate Gallery, the Beatles Experience, the Yellow Submarine in Chavasse Park, the police headquarters, the law courts, the fire station and the back streets from the Baltic Fleet to the Bluecoat and across to Mathew Street, the Cavern Club and the Town Hall! All this with the BBC Radio Merseyside studios in Paradise Street in the middle of it all!

On this first visit I returned at 8.20 with a tally of 16 species of birds (including the Liver Birds, of course!). Four species of gulls are winter residents on Merseyside: Herring Gulls and Lesser Blackbacks (the big ones); Common and Blackheaded Gulls (without their black heads in winter!). A Cormorant was diving on Albert Dock, quiet and serene at this time of the morning. As well as 'ordinary' pigeons, both Collared Dove and Woodpigeon were in the trees of the Moathouse garden, something you wouldn't have seen about ten years or so earlier as they had only moved into the city centre relatively recently. Similarly the Goldfinches, perhaps the highlight of the walk. A winter flock of about 25 of these beauties was feeding on the alders along the path across Chavasse Park, people walking past quite oblivious to them. I remember thinking if the same people saw Goldfinches on a TV nature programme they would be delighted to see these colourful birds, yet here they were, right over their very own heads! I had to resist the impulse to stop them, shake them and say "Look!" because I didn't want to get arrested – not on my first day!

About 20 Starlings were around Mann Island. Magpies and Mistle Thrushes were obviously nesting around Chavasse Park. I had already noticed a Mistle Thrush nest in January up on one of the tall lamp posts in the car park next to the law courts. Greenfinch (spring calls and song), Blackbird, Blue Tit and Pied Wagtail completed the list.

FERRY CROSS THE MERSEY: After I had reported back at 8.20 I took the ferry across to Seacombe. High tide had been at 5.09 and now there was plenty of shore exposed along the Mersey from Seacombe to New Brighton., Just below Wallasey Town Hall I found an Oystercatcher, a Curlew, at least 60 Redshank and 10 or more Turnstones. While I was there another man turned up with binoculars and started looking too. He said he was 'only' a beginner and I remember secretly wondering if he'd just been listening to BBC Radio Merseyside's Nature Watch broadcast and rushed out inspired to have a look himself!

A Nature Watch view of Prenton Park.

20 FEB: PRENTON PARK: Half Time: TRANMERE 0 SOUTHAMPTON 3

Full Time: TRANMERE 4 SOUTHAMPTON 3

Another part of the NATURE WATCH plan was to follow the major highlights of the Merseyside calendar to show that there are other things going on in the living space we share with so many other creatures and wildlife – all happening at the same time. A lot of people had the impression that you have to go to a nature reserve to see nature but we are still surrounded by it, even in a built-up area like Merseyside.

Even the few people who do not usually follow local football could not be help being captivated by the antics of Tranmere Rovers across the river from their premiership cousins at Goodison and Anfield. In fact to reach this stage of the FA Cup Tranmere had beaten (thrashed?!) Everton – at Goodison – in the previous round and now this incredible recovery against Southampton put Tranmere against Liverpool in the next round. With every kick Tranmere seemed to be rewriting the history books – only to be relegated at the end of the season!

The day after Tranmere's dream victory over Southampton I decided to go down to Prenton Park to see what it was like 'the morning after'. It may have been my imagination, but I was sure I could still hear the echoes of the cheers! There is a large area of allotments next to the Prenton Park football ground, many of them neglected which looked ideal, especially for butterflies later in the year. A group of pigeon fanciers told me about a Kestrel that nests there in a hole in a tree. There had been a big drop in the number of sparrows, no Bullfinches any more, but Grey Wagtails in winter. House Martins came to collect mud when they were building their nests, as well as more typical garden birds such as Robin, Wren, Hedge Sparrow, Blackbird, Goldfinch. At this time of the year a continuation from Prenton Park across to Victoria Park and Mersey Park in Tranmere proper did not reveal much more, most interesting a Goldcrest singing in the small group of pine trees in Victoria Park. Impressive views across the river to Liverpool.

Nature Watch at the Chinese New Year celebrations, always a major event in the Merseyside calendar.

Grey Wagtail territory, Canning Dock.

Canning Dock and the Albert Dock Complex

Albert-Kings Dock 'beach' at low tide

23 FEBRUARY: PIER HEAD TO PARADISE (STREET) NATURE TRAIL.
ALBERT DOCK AND CHAVASSE PARK

It was just on sunrise when I went out of the studio in Paradise Street at 7.00 to see what was going on outside. I could hardly believe my eyes when a Sparrowhawk flew low over Paradise Street bus station and through the gap of Cable Street into Derby Square, putting up a flock of alarmed pigeons. Only minutes before I had been telling listeners to look out for frightened flocks of pigeons or Starlings as a sign that a Sparrowhawk was about and here it was, happening before my own eyes. Instant confirmation that NATURE WATCH tips do work!

Collared Doves like to nest in evergreens where available. There is only one small fir tree in the Moathouse garden and sure enough, a Collared Dove had built its flimsy platform nest there, close to the slender trunk. At least one pair of Woodpigeons was also nesting somewhere close by and there were another ten 'visitors' out on the grass of Chavasse Park itself. The flock of Goldfinches was still there and in one of the trees by the Yellow Submarine I could see an old Goldfinch nest in the bare branches, confirmation that some of them stayed on to nest here. I couldn't help thinking that the Goldfinches had been attracted to this tree in particular because of the yellow of the submarine which was exactly the same tone as the yellow on the Goldfinch's wings! When I went back to the studio I sketched a quick cartoon for Linda (McDermott) showing baby Goldfinches in their nest singing: *We all live by a Yellow Submarine!*

There were three male Mallard on the slipway of Salthouse Dock – almost certainly a sign that three females were at nesting sites, possibly quite close at hand.

The tide was coming in (low tide: 5.52) but there was still some mud exposed at Canning Dock gates. A single Redshank was exploring the mud and a Carrion Crow flying over Albert Dock brought the grand total of birds on the Pier Head to Paradise (Street) Nature Trail to 20 species after two visits. There would obviously be more to come as the year progressed and I was already excited to know what would turn up.

BIRKENHEAD PARK: After reporting back at 8.20 I got the underground to Birkenhead Park to see if I could find any more Waxwings. They had recently been reported in the area, also in Upton. I didn't find any Waxwings but there was plenty going on. A Jay seemed to be having an argument with a Grey Squirrel. Coal Tits quite tame, expecting to be fed if you stood still for too long! A Nuthatch piping loud and clear and a Great Spotted Woodpecker. The Lower Park is just within 2 miles of the Pier Head, quite a bit closer than Sefton Park and it must be the site closest to the Pier Head for nesting Nuthatches, Woodpeckers and Tree Creepers. Long Tailed Tits at Birkenhead Park Station were probably already nest building in a gorse bush visible from passing trains.

BIDSTON DOCK: A pair of beautiful Great Crested Grebes was back on the pool at the end of Bidston Dock, only 2 ½ miles from the Pier Head. Since 1995 they have also been nesting on the lake in Walton Hall Park, 3 ½ miles from the Pier Head.

13

Left: Anglican Cathedral, nesting site of Kestrels and Ravens

Facing page: Hamilton Square Station, Birkenhead, nesting site of Peregrine Falcons

MARCH: RAVENS ON LIVERPOOL'S ANGLICAN CATHEDRAL

Of the many specialities on Merseyside the arrival of Ravens at Liverpool's Anglican Cathedral must rank as one of the greatest sensations of all. Ravens traditionally nest on cliffs and crags in mountainous and coastal areas, although on the Continent they do nest in big trees in forests and no doubt used to in Britain until they were persecuted into retreat. There had been no records at all of Ravens nesting on any sort of building until a pair took up residence on Chester Cathedral about six years ago now, where they have nested successfully ever since, sometimes using the Town Hall tower instead of the cathedral. It seemed only to be a matter of time before this trend would continue and in 1999 a pair of Ravens turned up at Liverpool's Anglican Cathedral, built a nest but did not lay eggs for some reason. In 2000 they did and in January 2001 they had starred on BBC TV in the 'Bill Oddie Goes Wild' special about Liverpool and the Merseyside region.

The Ravens stayed in the area and they were back at the cathedral early in the year showing all signs of nesting again. But when I went up to the cathedral at the beginning of March Maurice Bray, clerk of works, was obviously concerned that they hadn't been seen for a while. As I spoke to Simon, one of the staff, outside the cathedral a helicopter was circling overhead and Simon told me there had been quite a lot of helicopter activity those last few days which could have had something to do with the Ravens' disappearance. Would they come back? They were seen near the cathedral once or twice after that but had obviously given up on any plans for nesting. The question was: Where had they gone? A question we tried to answer as the year progressed.

2 MARCH: PIER HEAD TO PARADISE (STREET) NATURE TRAIL:

A Mistle Thrush was sitting on a nest in a tree just outside Canning Place fire station. The tide was out and about 50 Redshank had come onto the Albert Dock 'beach', a large expanse of sand and mud exposed at low tide off Albert Dock, Kings Dock, Queens Dock. A smaller wader was probably a Dunlin and in the distance I could see the tall silhouette of a Heron by the water's edge.

PEREGRINE FALCONS AT HAMILTON SQUARE STATION

The Peregrines at Hamilton Square Station had also featured in the 'Bill Oddie Goes Wild' programme on BBC TV in January. They had been nesting here for several years already but for 'security reasons' they had not been publicised before. A pair had also been nesting on the tobacco warehouse at Stanley Dock but were not successful until 2000 because the nest had previously always been washed out by rain.

On 10 March while most birdwatchers were at Parkgate watching the high tide which covered the marsh, and hoping to catch a glimpse of a hunting Peregrine, I had a pair to myself, circling, calling and courting just above my head around the tower at Hamilton Square Station!

The Peregrines – and the Ravens if they stayed – would obviously be amongst the stars of any Merseyside Nature Watch and so I decided to produce a small brochure which John McGowan at the station kiosk then offered to customers in aid of his Claire House collection.

3 MARCH: BIDSTON MOSS: More Coltsfoot in flower. A Woodcock (still there on 14 March). Alder catkins and pussy willow. Eight Lapwings, presumably planning to nest again, less than 3 miles from the Pier Head.

8 MARCH: VALE PARK, New Brighton: A beautiful display of Crocus. Stonechat at LEASOWE BAY. Celandine in flower in DIBBINSDALE, where both Green and Great Spotted Woodpecker were calling. Also 12 Teal on the flooded field there.

9 MARCH: PIER HEAD TO PARADISE (STREET) NATURE TRAIL: A pair of Canada Geese flew low along the Pier Head, looking up startled as the Liver Building clock struck 7.30! Great Tit and Hedge Sparrow brought the grand total of birds seen to 27.

*St George's Hall
and St John's
Gardens 2001 – not
a sparrow to be seen*

**10 MARCH:
BBC RADIO
MERSEYSIDE
LOCAL HISTORY
EXHIBITION AT
ST GEORGE'S
HALL**

In association with Liverpool City Council in aid of the BBC Radio Merseyside Charitable Trust running for two days, Saturday and Sunday. Amongst the fifty or more stands at the exhibition there were many which were of special interest to NATURE WATCH. It was very encouraging to see just how many local and voluntary initiatives there are, such as the Wavertree Society and Garston and District Historical Society, which not only take an interest in the past but also in the future and the local environment – for wildlife and people alike!

THE MYSTERY OF THE MISSING SPARROWS: After visiting the exhibition I had another look around St John's Gardens, the Museum and the Walker Art Gallery – in search of city centre House Sparrows. I was sure I used to see them here when I worked in the museum's Natural History Centre in the 1980s and earlier at the Pier Head too, but on my Friday walks about town and up to the Anglican Cathedral I had not found any at all. There was already alarm over the dramatic decline in sparrow numbers nationwide and there were several theories as to why. But it was still very much a mystery which had taken ornithologists by surprise because even the keenest of birdwatchers had rarely kept notes of sightings and numbers of House Sparrows, assuming them to be 'everywhere'. This was a situation where BBC Radio Merseyside's NATURE WATCH listeners could be of great assistance by reporting the presence – or absence – of sparrows in their own particular area.

13 MARCH: CANNING PLACE FIRE STATION: Three young Mistle Thrushes have flown the nest in the tree outside the fire station. We have gathered them up and put them round the corner for safety.   Andy Bailey, firefighter

14 MARCH: BUZZARD OVER HAMILTON SQUARE: While I was waiting to see if the Peregrines were about I spotted a large bird up in the sky. Yes, it was a Buzzard. I wasn't the only one who had spotted it. The male Peregrine suddenly appeared and flew up to confront the Buzzard and a dog fight ensued right over Hamilton Square, until the Buzzard drifted off towards Oxton. Keep an eye on the sky: you never know what might be up there !

16 MARCH NATURE WATCH NEWS

We started the BBC Radio Merseyside Nature Watch on Friday 16 February. I was able to give a picture of what had been going on since the beginning of the year. An overwintering Chiffchaff was out in the snow just after Christmas and twice in January I saw a winter Blackcap which even came out with a few phrases of song on sunny days in February and March.

Magpies were already working on nests at the end of December when there was also some Mistle Thrush song. Blackbirds and Song Thrushes were singing regularly from the end of January, joining Robins and Wrens which had been singing all winter, Hedge Sparrows since 9 January.

Winter Waxwings from Siberia arrived at the beginning of January and were seen in many locations on Merseyside through February and March. Redwings were seen regularly, not so many Fieldfares.

Two foxes were out frolicking in the sunshine on 24 Jan when a first garden Primula was seen in flower, Snowdrops from 8 Feb soon followed by Daffodils and Crocus. On 13 February in a warm spell around midday a Small Tortoiseshell butterfly was tempted out of hibernation, the only one so far.

By the end of February about 20 species of birds had been heard singing, if you include Collared Doves cooing and Carrion Crows crowing! Skylarks from 11 February, Chaffinches a little later.

A few Coltsfoot were in flower in February, then abundant in March, always the first wild flower to be appear. By 8 March alder catkins, pussy willow, blackthorn (which is white!) and Lesser Celandine were in flower, in all about 18 species of wild flowers, including those sometimes called 'weeds'! Some hawthorn bushes and honeysuckle were showing first leaves and the leaves of many other plants and flowers were starting to come through.

The first Chiffchaff song was heard on 11 March, possibly a bird which had overwintered, and first Wheatears had arrived on the coast by 16 March. Grey Wagtails were back in urban areas after the frost – one to watch out for, nesting in the most unlikely places – including a back yard in a busy shopping centre last year!

On 13 March three young Mistle Thrushes had already left their nest in Chavasse Park. Other birds had been seen collecting nest material: Blackbirds, Blue Tits, House Sparrows, Robin, Long Tailed Tits. By 16 March I had found six Long Tailed Tits' nests, confirming that they are increasing and spreading closer to the city centre. The nearest to the Pier Head are probably at the Anglican Cathedral. Where else?

By 16 March most of the Blackheaded Gulls had left playing fields and returned to their breeding colonies. Common Gulls usually stay a little longer and Lesser Blackbacked Gulls were returning from the Atlantic coast, though many now stay here for the winter. The 'dawn chorus' in the city centre is very much dominated by the cries and calls of Herring Gulls and Lesser Blackbacks, both nesting on city centre rooftops, a relatively recent development worth keeping an eye on.

*Eleanor Rigby,
Stanley Street,
looking down at the
only city centre
sparrow left!*

There was a very good response to my appeal for information about sparrows. This is only a small representative selection of the reports sent in by BBC Radio Merseyside listeners.

GATEACRE: You can see the House Sparrow story from my Garden Bird Watch statistics: common 1996-1997; zero in 1999 and now appearing to move into recovery this year, though I still only usually see them in ones and twos.   David Holland

GATEACRE PARK DRIVE: We moved here last August (2000) from Childwall where we had over a dozen sparrows. They nested all around. Now, only a mile away, we never see one House Sparrow. We have lots of other birds – but no House Sparrows or Starlings.   Norma Richardson

WAVERTREE: I've got sparrows in my garden; they wait for their breakfast every morning. It is lovely to see them in the bird bath.   Mrs E. Bone

WAVERTREE: We used to have a lot of sparrows and Blue Tits but sadly no more, only Magpies.   M. Lees

WEST DERBY: We have sparrows and regular visits from a Wren and a Robin. Also Blue Tits nesting in a box as well as the usual Blackbirds, Starlings (not so often recently), Magpies and Collared Doves.   Glynn Williams

WEST DERBY: I live near Croxteth Park and we used to have a family of sparrows coming into our garden every day, but now there are no sparrows visiting.

Heather Vaughan

TRANMERE-PRENTON PARK: I have no sparrows at all but my friend who lives only a few roads away always has lots of sparrows. I put bread out but there may be too many cats.   Mrs J. Wade

The reports from Wavertree, West Derby and Tranmere make interesting reading. They show that the sparrow population seems to have become very localised, plenty in one garden, none a few doors away even. They will of course head for gardens where food is put out regularly, perhaps leaving the impression that there are none just down the road!

UTTING AVENUE, LIVERPOOL 4: You were asking about knowledge of sparrows. I can tell you they seem to congregate on the bottom of the trolleys at the Asda supermarket in Utting Avenue. Why there I do not know but my daughter and I have seen them there. I never see them in my garden as I used to a few years ago when they were quite cheeky. I think Magpies keep them away.   Mrs E. M. Harper

GARSTON: We have about 12 sparrows in our garden and have got two pairs which nest in the roof. It is lovely to hear them chirruping away.   Mr and Mrs Thomas

PENNY LANE: I live in a Victorian terrace near Penny Lane. I haven't seen any sparrows since around 1995. They used to sit on the yard wall and we had a local one – called Charlie – who used to bring his family to see us for about four years. I do miss the sparrows but at least the washing can blow unstained now – they always managed to hit something white!   Margaret Thompson

BEECHWOOD, Birkenhead: We have 12-15 sparrows in our garden which we have watched for generations. It is lovely when you see them feeding their young.

Earl McGliney

UPTON, Wirral: I have quite a flock of sparrows. They nest under the ivy on one wall and behind the cotoneaster on the garage wall.   Rosaline Jane

HESWALL: I still have sparrows, also Blackbirds, Thrushes, Robins, Tits, Finches, Magpies and greedy Starlings.   Mrs C. Stewart

THORNTON HOUGH: When I first came to live here 37 years ago the garden was full of sparrows but over the last 10-15 years they have just disappeared.

Mrs T. Helsby

BURSCOUGH: We have Starlings, Magpies, Blackbirds, Woodpigeon, a Sparrowhawk which we have seen twice – but no sparrows.   Mrs B. Jones

The last two reports suggest that it is not only in city centres but also in more rural areas where sparrows have been hardest hit, leaving the suburbs as the sparrow's main stronghold. When I saw the Albert Dock and city centre streets being sprayed with weed-killer later in the year I wondered whether this could be a reason why there are no sparrows at all left in the city centre where alternative food sources could be scanty. The only city centre sparrow I had seen was the one being fed by Eleanor Rigby in Stanley Street!

Then on 23 March after the Nature Watch broadcast I eventually found the first sparrows – in Cathedral Walk just below the Metropolitan Cathedral – and just within a mile of the Pier Head. They were in trees next to the flats there where they are no doubt fed by caring residents.

16 MARCH: UPTON, Wirral: Magpies have started building a nest in a tree behind my back wall. Last year the nest was next door but one but they pulled that one to pieces last week.   Rosaline Jane

I think if you had been able to watch their antics more closely, Rosaline, you would have found that the Magpies were not simply pulling the old nest to pieces. They were almost certainly moving house – quite literally - taking the twigs from the old nest to build the new one. Much easier than having all the bother and discomfort of breaking off fresh thorny twigs from a hawthorn or the like!

17 MARCH: BIDSTON MOSS: First real Lapwing display, obviously planning to nest again, 2½ miles from the Pier Head. Later in the year Lapwings were also reported nesting at Twelve Quays just a mile across the river from the Pier Head, also on the site of the old Clarence Dock power station.

By now I had found six Long Tailed Tits' nests. Putting out white feathers helped locate most of them as they were usually snapped up very quickly and taken to the nest to be used as lining. But if they were not yet ready to line the nest they would pick up the feather and remove it to a safe distance so as not to betray the nest site to potential predators.

HOYLAKE: First Wheatears reported along the coast. Little Gulls and Mediterranean Gull at Seaforth Nature Reserve.

18 MARCH: Snow shower around 14.00. Nevertheless Skylarks singing. Blue Tits performing their gliding display flight.

19 MARCH: WALLASEY VILLAGE: Burst of Blackcap song by the Cheshire Cheese from a bird which had overwintered in the area. A remarkable record of a Red Legged Partridge which flew out of the undergrowth – 'like a Woodcock' – from Heathbank, Breck Road.

I had found cassette tape hanging on a tree where Mistle Thrushes were nesting. I had assumed it was the work of some boys with the help of the wind perhaps and carefully removed it. Next day there was more cassette tape hanging by the nest and it was only then that I realised it must have been the Mistle Thrush itself which was bring the tape as nest material but had the same problem as many humans trying to handle it! Hence the streamers hanging from the nest. Plastic and blue string are also very fashionable.

20 MARCH: HALEWOOD CAR FACTORY: Bob the Birdman was talking about Blackbirds and other birds that sing in the dark. Well, come down here and have a walk around the outside of the Ford factory at 2 or 3 am any morning. You will hear birds singing and I have seen Kestrels flying around. The factory is lit up like a city centre and the birds think it's daytime. I don't know how they sleep.

Joe Carter

21 MARCH: PAUL McCARTNEY - *BLACKBIRD SINGING*

Fans flock to catch a glimpse of Sir Paul at the launch of his book 'Blackbird Singing'

Paul had chosen 21 March to launch his book because it was the fortieth anniversary of the Beatles' first evening 'gig' at the Cavern. It was also officially the first day of spring but the squalls of wet snow made it an uncomfortable wait for the many fans who had come to see him. BBC Radio Merseyside's Angela Heslop caught up with Paul for an interview at the Everyman that evening.

Paul claims the title is symbolic and the song is really about a black girl but I still believe that the inspiration came when he was returning home late one night and found it strange to hear a Blackbird singing in the artificial light of the street lamp just down the road from his house in Forthlin Road. My story and I'm sticking to it!

A few years earlier I had published my own collection of nature poetry which included one about real Blackbirds singing. Linda (McDermott) read it out during the Friday Nature Watch broadcast:

It starts in the dark/ melodious warbling in the air/ like soft waves lapping/ in gentle ripples/ falling on some distant shore/ growing louder still unseen/ until it's coming from all sides/ and by the time the first light shows/ the song is filling all the skies/ Before the people's day begins/ a morning hour at dawn/ they rule this world, this world is theirs/ as another day is born.

23 MARCH: WEST KIRBY: There always seems to be something going on in our garden – and lovely songs – at the moment from the Blackbird just outside the living room singing away every evening.   Irene and Edmund Jelley

23 MARCH: BOOTLE: We have been landscaping a section of the canal behind our premises in Brasenose Road. We did all the work ourselves with the assistance of a local landscape gardener who gave his time free of charge. Mersey Forest gave us a small grant and some trees and bluebells. We've had our local MP and councillors down to see it but 'as usual' no financial help is forthcoming. I will keep you up to date on this year's progress.   Kevin McNulty

**25 MARCH
SUNDAY
NATURE WATCH
PEREGRINE
FALCONS AT
HAMILTON
SQUARE
STATION**
*Peregrine
territory: Woodside's
many towers*

I invited listeners to join me at Hamilton Square Station at 10.00 to see the now 'famous' Peregrines which were nesting there – a bit of a gamble because there was no solid guarantee that they would show up! As it turned out we only had to wait about 20 minutes for good views of both birds circling in full view quite low for several minutes.

Then I suggested a taste of urban nature watching and soon we were walking along streets and back alleys to see what we could find. Ivy-Leaved Toadflax and Red Valerian were already in flower: the books say not until May so this could have had something to do with the urban 'micro-climate'. I showed the group the Mistle Thrush and Long Tailed Tit nests I had found earlier. The Mistle Thrush nest was in the fork of a tree only about six feet from the ground and next to a path, but so well camouflaged that hardly anybody ever noticed it. There was local history, of course, as well as natural history and I was satisfied at the end of the walk that the group had appreciated this way of looking at places, places that they felt they already knew, but surprised by how much there was to see that they hadn't noticed before.

NATIONAL EXHIBITION OF WILDLIFE ART AT THE PIER HEAD

It was an added bonus to have the National Exhibition of Wildlife Art at the Road Range Gallery, Mann Island – right in the middle of our Pier Head to Paradise (Street) Nature Trail!

Record numbers of animal and art lovers visited the National Exhibition of Wildlife Art which was being held in Liverpool for the third year and which is now acknowledged as a world beater. More than 400 works of art were on display. According to the organiser David Wilson the show is the largest open exhibition of wildlife art outside London and arguably the biggest in the UK.

"Wildlife habitats are continually disappearing through man-made developments and pollution. Many animals and birds are in danger of extinction because of our greed. This exhibition drives home the message that we are in danger of losing so much."

22

31 MARCH: NATURE WATCH NEWS

Two weeks since our last Nature Watch News and things have already moved on a lot in the meantime. Three young Mistle Thrushes had already flown the nest on 13 March and others are building nests or sitting. Wood Anemones have joined the Lesser Celandine in woodlands and the first beautiful pink cherry blossom was in flower by the end of the month.

I saw my first bat of the year at dusk on 28 March and on 30 March a Small Tortoiseshell butterfly, the first since the 'freak' one on 13 February. Watch out for Peacocks and Commas as well as Small Tortoiseshells coming out of hibernation; also Whites and Speckled Woods.

I found a hedgehog on 15 March – squashed on the road – the first victim of the year. Lots of frogspawn in the salt marsh at Red Rocks, Hoylake. Chiffchaffs are singing regularly now, so we can start to expect other early migrants, even Swallows.

On 20 March and again on 26 March there was a very big movement of Meadow Pipits over Merseyside. Apparently 3000 were counted passing at Hilbre Island on the Dee but they were also passing over your house! They will continue to do so for some time, so watch and listen out for little brown birds which go 'fit, fit-fit'. They are returning from milder lowlands to the hills and moors.

At the Anglican Cathedral the Ravens have been coming and going since February. The pair at Chester Cathedral have eggs now, so we can only wait and see what happens in Liverpool. After finding no House Sparrows at all from the Pier Head to the Anglican Cathedral I asked listeners to report whether they had sparrows or not in their area. A big Thank You to the many people who did. We were able to confirm that sparrows are still in the city suburbs but much more locally than in the days when they used to be 'everywhere'. On 23 March I found sparrows in Cathedral Walk just below the Metropolitan Cathedral, as close as they come now, it seems, to the city centre. More reports always welcome to fill in the picture in more detail.

With House Sparrows and Meadow Pipits as the latest additions we now have a grand total of 36 species on the City Centre bird list which includes Chaffinch, Song Thrush, Kestrel, Long Tailed Tit – and the Ravens – all seen around the Anglican Cathedral. Our Pier Head to Paradise (Street) Nature Trail can be extended, of course, to include the Mersey itself on our 'Ferry Cross the Mersey' cruises to see waders on the shore at Seacombe and Egremont and the Peregrines at Woodside and Hamilton Square, all within a mile of the Pier Head!

MARCH FLOWERS: Coltsfoot, Lesser Celandine, Gorse, Crocus, Primrose, Daffodil, Dandelion, Speedwell, Daisy, Red Dead Nettle, Shepherd's Purse, Chickweed, Wood Anemone, Dog's Mercury, Marsh Marigold, Periwinkle, Hairy Bittercress, Whitlow Grass.

GREETINGS TO BBC RADIO MERSEYSIDE NATURE WATCH:

Dear Bob, Spring is here and Meadow Pipits are migrating over Hampstead. Also first Chiffchaffs and Wheatears have appeared. Good luck!   Bill Oddie

1ST APRIL:
SUNDAY
NATURE
WATCH -
FERRY
CROSS
THE
MERSEY

The river is, of course, the heart and soul of Merseyside and together with our Pier Head to Paradise (Street) Nature Trail I was keen to make it the focal point of our BBC Radio Merseyside NATURE WATCH. I cannot think of anywhere else with so many waders, seabirds and ducks on a river that has so much dockland, industry and housing along its banks as the Mersey has.

Last year on 1 April the Liver Bird laid a huge egg, found on the ground below. None this year but standing in Chavasse Park by the fire station I noticed that one of the Liver Birds had flown across to the top of the tunnel ventilation shaft! (Go and have a look yourself if you don't believe me!)

We took the 10 o'clock ferry across to Seacombe where we had good views of Oystercatchers and Redshanks on the shore. Linnets and Pied Wagtail were both showing signs of nesting. Then we took the ferry to Woodside. The Peregrines didn't turn up this time but a Small Tortoiseshell brightened up the day and later the first Peacock butterfly of the year was seen out of hibernation.

2 APRIL: Bluebells ready to burst into flower. Sand Martins in several places.

3 APRIL: Blackcap song. Another Peacock and more Sand Martins. Magnolia out.

5 APRIL: Blackbirds collecting nest material. Starlings going into nesting holes.

6 APRIL: PIER HEAD TO PARADISE (STREET) NATURE TRAIL: A Mistle Thrush had been sitting on a second brood for at least a week now. Greenfinch display flight and song. A Grey Wagtail was still around Canning Dock, also seen flying past the law courts.

7 APRIL: First Cowslips in flower. Cowslips are one of the most popular wild flowers which have been re-introduced in many places on Merseyside where natural regeneration projects are being carried out. Others are Red Campion, Ox-Eye Daisy, Knapweed, Scabious, Meadow Cranesbill, Wild Carrot, Melilot, Kidney Vetch.

**8 APRIL:
SUNDAY NATURE
WATCH
GRAND NATIONAL
SPECIAL AT AINTREE
RACECOURSE**

In keeping with our plan to follow the major events of the Merseyside calendar on our Sunday Nature Watches we had the unique opportunity of exploring the Grand National course, famous the world over, the very next day after the big race.

As we stood on the Melling Road where the horses had stampeded past less than 24 hours earlier several Skylarks were singing above our heads having somehow survived the disturbance of the previous days. Following the canal from Anchor Bridge to Canal Turn we saw Swans, Coots and Moorhens all nesting and a Heron flew past. We heard both Blackcap and Chiffchaff singing from the bushes between Canal Turn and Beecher's Brook. Song Thrush and Hedge Sparrow were also singing. Very noticeable in the bare trees dotted around the racecourse were the many Magpie nests.

We had no fallers and we all completed the course, though it did take us nearly four hours just to go round once! By the end of the walk we had clocked up just on 30 species of birds – one for each fence!

9 APRIL: First reports of Swallows by BBC Radio Merseyside Nature Watch listeners though one or two had already been sighted elsewhere around the end of March.

LISCARD, Wallasey: The Grey Wagtail has been back at the nest site in our back yard – between Woolworth's and Boots in Liscard shopping centre.   Lenny Hoare

10 APRIL: First Comma butterfly out of hibernation. Another Peacock and at least five Small Tortoiseshells. A pair of Canada Geese planning to nest at Bidston Dock pool 2 ½ miles from the Pier Head. Also Partridge.

11 APRIL: ANGLICAN CATHEDRAL: Maurice Bray told me that there had been no sign of the Ravens at the cathedral for some time now. Starlings mating. A first wasp. Two more Swallows.

FERRY CROSS THE MERSEY: There was only a single Blackheaded Gull following the ferry now. The others had all returned to their breeding colonies – on the Ribble and Dee marshes or on inland meres and flashes.

15 APRIL: EASTER SUNDAY AT THE TWO CATHEDRALS

Easter Sunday was the logical time of the year to put the two Liverpool cathedrals on the NATURE WATCH map. The Anglican Cathedral with its Ravens and Kestrels usually got most of the ornithological glory but the first city centre House Sparrows had been found in Cathedral Walk, just below the Metropolitan Cathedral, and so honours could now be shared!

We had hoped, but not really expected, to find the Ravens back, but there was ample compensation in the form of a 'dog-fight' between the local Kestrel and a visiting Peregrine round the cathedral tower to the accompaniment of the sonorous cathedral bells – an unforgettable experience. Long Tailed Tits were obviously nesting in a bush on the Gambier Terrace side of St James' 'sunken' cemetery.

It was a rather cold, windy and rainy morning (almost sleet) and so I continued on my own to Mossley Hill to check out the possibility that the Ravens had moved to that part of Liverpool. No sign of Ravens but a beautiful display of daffodils in Sefton Park. So you don't have to go to Wordsworth's Lake District to see daffodils " beside the lake beneath the trees, fluttering and dancing in the breeze." It was all happening in Sefton Park!

The cheeky heron in Sefton Park

I was also lucky enough to see a Tree Creeper disappear into a crevice in the trunk of an old birch tree where it was building its nest. Nuthatches and Great Spotted Woodpeckers also conspicuous. A tame, almost cheeky Heron was fishing in the bandstand lake. Later in the year Neil Farrell sent in a photo of a Heron in Sefton Park – presumably the same cheeky bird. Moorhens and Coots also nesting – often in dangerously exposed places.

15 APRIL: GARSTON: It's been a good year for frogs and I now have plenty of tadpoles. On Easter Monday there was a bright blue butterfly in my garden. Could this have been a Holly Blue?
Kathy Andrews

Yes, I'm sure it was – and the earliest reported in 2001 which turned out to be a good year for Holly Blues – so thank you, Kathy!

WEST KIRBY: We live in an old Victorian semi and have always had butterflies hibernating – but our neighbours, no. (They think we must be peculiar!) Once we counted 47 nestling in corners, stuck to the back of wardrobes, under beds! Why just our house? Is it a known B&B for butterflies?!

Irene and Edmund Jelley

15 APRIL: NATURE WATCH NEWS

As predicted, Peacocks and Commas, as well as Small Tortoiseshell butterflies have all been seen out of hibernation now. After a week of wet weather most types of trees were ready to burst into full leaf. Cowslips and first Bluebells were out along with a few other common wild flowers. In gardens beautiful Magnolia; berberis bushes golden yellow with the buds of their flowers. A Red-Tailed Bumble Bee on 8 April as well as the 'normal' sort. A first wasp on 11 April.

After Chiffchaffs and Wheatears, now also Willow Warblers, singing regularly since 9 April. A few Sand Martins seen passing through and on 11 April I saw my first two Swallows (enough to make a summer?!). A few had already been reported earlier at the end of March. Blackcaps which stayed for the winter as reported by many listeners have probably been joined by true summer migrants by now.

Grey Wagtails have been seen back at their nesting site in a back yard in Liscard shopping centre, Wallasey. They are nesting in many other city and dockland locations. I've seen them passing over Chavasse Park to and from Albert Dock and I'm hoping to be able to track down their nesting site but it will be a needle in a haystack job! Where else have they been seen?

Magpie nest, Liscard, Wallasey. Grey Wagtails nest in the yard behind Woolies (in the background.)

The Peregrines can be seen regularly now around Hamilton Square and Woodside Ferry. But the Ravens haven't been seen at the Anglican Cathedral for some time now.

Garden birds are busy building nests or sitting on eggs already and in the next week or so when wind and weather are favourable we can expect the first big influx of summer migrants: more Swallows, Blackcaps and Willow Warblers, Whitethroats and Sedge Warblers. Also watch out for Redstarts which often turn up in gardens on their travels, if only for a fleeting visit. And Common Sandpipers should be turning up at lakes and reservoirs soon.

16 APRIL: First Small White butterfly of the year. More Tortoiseshells. Remains of a Redshank found below Peregrine nest site at Hamilton Square Station.

Steve Capstick, BBC TV cameraman

17 APRIL: WEST KIRBY: My husband is at this moment chasing away a Magpie from attacking 'our' songster Blackbird's nest in the hedge, but what can we do?…oh, now there's chicken wire being placed over the hedge – hope the chair doesn't collapse under him (husband not Magpie!). Irene Jelley

BLACKBIRDS NESTING IN QUIGGINS, CITY CENTRE: When I walked into this unique 'Old Curiosity Shop' in College Lane next to the Bluecoat, I was surprised to hear the noise of young Blackbirds. I found them – two – sitting on a pipe at the side of the showrooms. The mother soon appeared, fed one, then disappeared through a gap between the wall and the corrugated roof, returning the same way a minute or two later. The boys in Quiggins showed me the cupboard where they had nested and another bird was still sitting on a second nest high up on a girder. In the past they have nested in the baskets of bicycles hanging from the roof and even on the chimney pot of a doll's house!

19 APRIL: BIDSTON DOCK POOL: First Common Sandpiper of the year. Long Tailed Tits sitting on eggs. Alkanet in flower. A Peacock and more Tortoiseshells.

20 APRIL: PIER HEAD TO PARADISE (STREET) NATURE TRAIL: There was a Willow Warbler singing from the trees by the law courts on Chavasse Park, the first – and only - true summer migrant that was to be seen here, but symbolic of the arrival of summer visitors all over Merseyside which was now starting to get underway.

A Grey Wagtail was on the quayside by the tug *Brocklebank* in Canning Dock which then flew across to the lock gates by the pilot boat *Edmund Gardner*, singing and showing general breeding behaviour. It was still there about an hour later.

LISCARD, Wallasey: Still Grey Wagtails: the pair nesting in Liscard shopping centre have car parks and flat rooftops to feed on in the mornings before people and traffic appear and it only takes a minute to fly down to the lake in Central Park where they are also seen regularly. There is real magic in this story. The Grey Wagtails nest in a back yard where there used to be an old, deep well, but which was blocked up many years ago, well before Grey Wagtails had started moving into city and urban areas away from their traditional nesting sites in more idyllic 'old mill by the stream' surroundings. The Grey Wagtails must know somehow that there is water down there, but how?! Our urban and dockland Grey Wagtails are just as much a Merseyside speciality as the Ravens and the Peregrines.

BIRKENHEAD PARK: Five more Willow Warblers singing after the one in Chavasse Park that morning. Nuthatch nest hole in a tree by a street lamp.

21 APRIL: First Speckled Wood butterfly of the year. First migrant Whitethroat.

First family of 8 tiny Mallard ducklings.

HARRISON DRIVE, Wallasey: Fifty migrating Sandwich Terns resting on the sand by the coast guard station. House Martins back early at traditional nesting site at the corner of Grove Road.

The cupboard in Quiggins -
(Blackbird's nest)

Mistle Thrush on nest, next to
Law Courts

Robin's nest site under old carpet (in foreground)

Top left: 'De Wadden', Canning Dock, Blackbird's nest site

Top right: The Blackbird's nest below decks

Herring Gulls now nest on the chimney pots of the Port of Liverpool building

30

SUNDAY 22 APRIL : CHILDWALL WOODS AND FIELDS

We linked up with the Friends of Childwall Woods and Fields for their spring bird watch led by Shaun Wilson who wrote:

The Woods were quite productive, with good sightings of Jay, Great Spotted Woodpecker, Nuthatch, Tree Creeper, Long Tailed Tit and Chiffchaff. The Chiffchff was our only warbler sighting and it was excellent to be able to demonstrate first hand to the group the difference between the Chiffchaff call and that of the Great Tit.

Unfortunately the Blackcap, our other woodland warbler which arrived and had been seen and heard two weeks earlier was neither heard nor seen on the day of the bird watch.

The fields were less productive with a disappointing lack of Whitethroats which had not arrived yet or were hiding in the bramble scrub because of the miserable weather. However, we did see a pair of Sparrowhawks soaring over the top field and some Willow Warblers could be heard in the plantation on the middle field. A mixed flock of Linnet and Goldfinch was seen flying over the top field.

The commoner birds spotted were Chaffinch, Great Tit, Blue Tit, Magpie, Woodpigeon, Carrion Crow, Jackdaw, Song Thrush, Blackbird, Robin, Hedge Sparrow and Wren. The Song Thrush was particularly appealing because it put out a chorus usually reserved for dusk, with repeated phrases echoing around the woods.

Three Grey Squirrels were seen in the tree canopy and a Nuthatch was seen entering a nesting hole in a large sweet chestnut tree with one of the squirrels foraging in the branches above. This caused the Nuthatch to issue an alarm call.

At the end of the walk I showed the group two or three new Wren nests that we had found this spring. The two Wren nests in Childwall Woods were cleverly hidden low down in the woodland fringe. The Wren's nest in Black Woods is a classic because it is in the roots of a large upturned tree.

Another highlight of the day was the Stock Dove seen inspecting a large nest hole in an old tree – certainly one of the specialities of the woods, one of the few places where Stock Doves still nest on Merseyside – here about 5 ½ miles from the Pier Head.

23 APRIL: A total of 9 Swallows seen during the day. Robin feeding young in a nest under a piece of old carpet draped over allotment railings. Coot with one egg at BIDSTON DOCK pool. First ladybird.

24 APRIL: WEST DERBY: BBC Radio Merseyside's Travel Watch expert Ron Davies was kept awake by the hooting of a Tawny Owl. Bluebells, Garlic Mustard or Jack-by-the-Hedge. More Swallows.

BIDSTON DOCK POOL: The Coot's egg from the previous day had already been predated. Probably the fox which hunted here regularly. Young Moorhens and Coots hardly ever seen as a result. The pair of Great Crested Grebes had started building a floating nest platform at the edge of the reeds. First Sedge Warbler.

31

SUMMER VISITORS ARRIVE ON MERSEYSIDE

25 APRIL: More Swallows, Sedge Warblers, Whitethroats, Wheatears, Common Sandpiper. First Grasshopper Warbler (also reported earlier at Red Rocks, Hoylake and later at Childwall Fields). Blackcaps carrying nest material into undergrowth –all this happening within three miles of the Pier Head.

BIDSTON DOCK POOL: It was a surprise to find a Coot sitting on the nest platform which the Great Crested Grebes had made. They were now trying to reclaim it from the Coot which remained steadfast and later started building its own nest on top of the very useful foundation provided by the grebes. We nearly always expect human intervention e.g. vandalism to be the cause of such nesting failures but in this case it was local Coots.

26 APRIL: BBC RADIO MERSEYSIDE, PARADISE STREET: There was a panic in reception: we were being invaded by ants, not exactly favourites with reception and cleaning staff. Tony Snell invited listeners to phone in with remedies which only added to the mirth and confusion, whilst I was trying to defend them as one of nature's wonders – which did little for my popularity!

Producer Graham White drew my attention to a story in the Daily Post about a pair of Mistle Thrushes nesting in the BASF factory at Seacombe which had led to the postponement of a building project there. (Ironically the thrushes may have saved the company a lot of money: a few weeks later the factory went up in flames leading to its closure.) Red Campions coming into flower. More Small Tortoiseshells and another Peacock.

172 PAIRS OF TERNS NESTING JUST FOUR MILES FROM THE PIER HEAD:

Terns, also known as sea swallows, are magnificent and graceful birds which return every spring from as far away as West Africa, Antarctica even, to nest in Britain. Since the pools and nature reserve were created at Seaforth at the mouth of the Mersey Common Terns have been staying to nest – from 1986 onwards. They nest on specially made rafts and in 2001 a record number of 172 pairs were counted – forgivably noisy during the breeding season!

LITTLE GULLS – ANOTHER MERSEYSIDE SPECIALITY:

Every spring there is a big passage of Little Gulls on the Mersey as they head back to their breeding grounds in Holland, Denmark and the Baltic. First reports came in March and in April a record number of over 800 were counted at Crosby Marina and Seaforth where they traditionally congregate before moving on. Birds flying in to join them were seen on several occasions from the ferry between Seacombe and the Pier Head. We have four 'regular' species of gulls on Merseyside: the big Herring and Lesser Blackbacked Gulls and the smaller Common and Blackheaded Gulls – both of which disappear to their breeding grounds in spring. The Little Gulls are unmistakable: black heads like the Blackheaded Gulls, but smaller and very white, contrasting with the dark underwings. Their 'floating' flight is also very characteristic.

We said that we would keep you informed about new ducklings on our canal bank. We have seen two lots of ducklings, one with twelve, one with seven. The canal bank looks really good now with all the trees and flowers we have planted all starting to bloom.

Kevin McNulty

PIER HEAD TO PARADISE (STREET) NATURE TRAIL: The Grey Wagtail was still at Canning Dock by the pilot boat *Edmund Gardner* and I was confident they were going to nest somewhere on or around the lock gate, though I hadn't seen any signs of nest building.

A pair of Shelduck flew up river off Albert Dock and later a pair of Canada Geese flew over the Pier Head, continuing inland possibly towards Sefton Park or even further.

NETHERTON: A family of hedgehogs lives in the ivy on the ground just outside my back window. I hear them more than I see them. They can be very noisy around dusk!

Shirley Hudson

CHILDWALL WOODS: *In the period 29 April-1 May we received two reports of owls being mobbed by Crows and Magpies. In one incident two baby owls were involved. One was on its back being pecked: the other was standing close by, terrified. The mother was circling overhead trying to distract the attackers.*

The attackers retreated on the approach of three of our lady members. One picked up the baby owl and evacuated it from the open ground to the shrubbery, giving it time to recover. Finally, with great effort, both baby birds managed to fly off low, hopefully to join their mother. It is not recommended to pick up baby birds in distress, but this, surely, was the exception to the rule. It was clear that the baby owl would have died otherwise.

Newsletter: Friends of Childwall Woods and Fields

SUNDAY 29 APRIL BIDSTON MOSS

Bidston Dock Pool with Storyteller's Chair in the form of a heron

It was National Census Day (once every ten years) but while others were asking how many people there were, we made our own census, not of the number of people, but of the birds and how many species we could find. Having seen just about every species of summer warbler that could be expected around the Bidston Moss area in the previous ten days this was the ideal opportunity to invite Nature Watch listeners to familiarise themselves with the various songs and calls of these and other summer visitors. En route to our meeting place at Bidston Station (10.00 as always) I had already seen my first Swift of the year and found first Reed Warblers at the pools by the station, always a few days later than the Sedge Warblers which were already settling in. From the railway bridge we could see the Crow's nest (nothing maritime - a real one!) up on the pylon and the Blue Tit flew into the end of the pipe on the telephone mast about 30 ft above the ground where it was nesting again. House Martins were sailing round over the pools and we were able to pick out Chiffchaff and Willow Warbler song as well as Blackcap and Whitethroat. The Lesser Whitethroat I had seen here a few days earlier let us down but the Grasshopper Warbler was there, reeling its uncanny mechanical song at the back of the B&Q warehouse. Seven species of warbler in all and 38 species for the day. That list included another Common Sandpiper at Bidston Dock pool along with the Great Crested Grebes, Moorhens, Coots and Canada Geese which were nesting there. No Swans this year after failing last year. Also good views of Sparrowhawk and Long Tailed Tits.

THE NATIONAL WILD FLOWER CENTRE: Merseyside might seem an unlikely place to 'outsiders' to have the National Wild Flower Centre. But it's here – in Court Hey Park, Huyton. It was founded in 1995 with the help of a lottery Millennium Fund grant to demonstrate the creative conservation techniques pioneered in Knowsley – that's what it says in the brochure.

Along with the annual National Exhibition of Wildlife Art at the Pier Head this already puts Merseyside at the forefront of national wildlife initiatives and lends great support to our aim of turning Merseyside into the first Metropolitan Wildlife Park in the country!

34

30 APRIL: NATURE WATCH NEWS

The first big influx of summer migrants arrived overnight on 24-25 April. Sedge Warblers and Whitethroats had arrived, more Willow Warblers, Blackcaps and Wheatears. And a nice surprise was to find several Grasshopper Warblers which were still present at the end of the month. After two on 11 April and four on 17 April Swallows were seen daily from 21 April, when two House Martins were already back at their nest site – earlier than usual.

Three Swifts were seen flying together on 29 April, when first Reed Warblers were in the reeds, a few days after the Sedge Warblers as is usually the case. Common Sandpipers were reported on three days in April, the first on 19 April. The big influx of migrants on 25 April was about five days later than last year, no doubt because of the weather situation, but they will quickly make up on those few 'lost' days. A female Redstart turned up on 30 April.

Small Tortoiseshell butterflies have been seen on all suitable days since 30 March, similarly Peacocks though in smaller numbers as always. Only one Comma so far – on 10 April. Small Whites were seen on four days from 16 April when the first Holly Blue was also reported. After one on 21 April Speckled Woods were becoming regular and daily by the end of the month, when there were plenty of Bluebells, Cowslips and Red Campions, also a lot of Garlic Mustard or Jack-by-the-Hedge. Lady's Smock and Oxford Ragwort also in flower.

There was a first ladybird on 23 April when I also noticed first ants. Another wasp was out on 26 April – all things to look forward to during the summer months! In gardens the red currant and forsythia which had been so conspicuous through April was starting to fade and tulips were taking over from daffodils. Magnolia and cherry blossom.

I saw a first family of eight ducklings on 21 April, around the same time as last year when BBC Radio Merseyside reported a family of ducklings walking down the main road towards to Wallasey Tunnel entrance!

Two pairs of Blackbirds are nesting in Quiggins again, Liverpool's unique 'Old Curiosity Shop' in College Lane next to the Bluecoat. This year they are nesting in a cupboard on display and up on a girder. In the past they have nested in the basket of a bicycle hanging from the roof and on the chimney pot of a giant doll's house!

Since 23 April I've been watching a pair of Robins feeding young in a nest under a piece of old carpet draped over railings in local allotments. By the end of the month most of the Long Tailed Tits were also feeding young in the nest. Blue Tits on the other hand hadn't even laid eggs. Great Spotted Woodpeckers and Nuthatches are nesting in Birkenhead Park, Childwall Woods and Sefton Park where I also found a Tree Creeper's nest on 15 April. On 26 April I saw a first Coot chick but found another dead away from the water, almost certainly the fox. And Magpies are prowling. I found a 'stolen' Song Thrush egg on 29 April. The first tragedies of spring.

*Ormskirk:Kes in
Thelma's garden*

1 MAY: ORMSKIRK: "Can you tell me the life span of a Kestrel? I have been feeding one in my garden for about 9-10 years now. She comes down for liver and chicken and I have also surprised her on the bird table attached to the kitchen window sill. Each year she brought four chicks, however I don't think she has a brood this year as she is still coming for food.

Poor thing, she is becoming senile (like the rest of us!). Sometimes she misses her footing when aiming for the garden seat and her wing doesn't fold back tidily. At this moment she is sunning herself on the garden archway. Sitting next to her is a Blackbird. She takes no notice of it at all."   Thelma Westell

I contacted Ron Billingsley in Huyton who has had a lot of experience with Kestrels and he estimates that the life span of a Kestrel is 'around ten years, maybe a little more' Thelma's Kestrel had probably only survived this long thanks to her liver and chicken.

WEST KIRBY: First Orange-Tip butterfly. Great Spotted Woodpecker and Nuthatch in Ashton Park. Fine display of Alexanders at the West Kirby end of the Wirral Way – "rather rare, usually by the sea". Hedge Sparrow feeding young in nest.

2 MAY: Another Orange-Tip; Peacock, Tortoiseshell, Speckled Wood and first Large White. Wheatear at Bidston Dock. Song Thrush heard bashing snails against its 'anvil' stone in amongst bushes. Blue Tit feeding partner as if practising for the many mouths it would be feeding in the coming weeks!

3 MAY: BIDSTON DOCK: Eight Wheatears all close together not far from the pool at the end of the dock – a beautiful picture. First Lady's Smock (Cuckoo Flower) and Kidney Vetch coming into flower.

36

The Bluecoat courtyard, a green oasis in the busy city centre

BLUECOAT CHAMBERS AND COURTYARD: Just round the corner from BBC BBC Radio Merseyside in College Lane, the Bluecoat courtyard is a haven for many birds such as Mistle Thrushes, Blackbirds, Great Tits, Blue Tits and Robins. Up on the roof are two (plastic) Eagle Owls, now ineffective deterrents to local pigeons! The Bluecoat is renowned for its Queen Anne architecture but the four magnificent London Planes at the entrance are probably the greatest natural monuments in the city.

4 MAY: PIER HEAD TO PARADISE (STREET) NATURE TRAIL: It was already clear that both Herring Gulls and Lesser Blackbacks must have been nesting on city centre rooftops for several years now. I was given concrete proof as I watched a Herring Gull ripping up tufts of grass near the Museum of Liverpool Life and flying up to a chimney pot on the Port of Liverpool Building just across the way on the other side of Mann Island. They have already 'invaded' most towns on the east and south coasts and in Wales. Merseyside visitors to Conwy and Llandudno will know that they can be quite a nuisance – 'sandwich snatchers'!

Starlings were feeding young in the mast lights of the pilot boat *Edmund Gardner* and I was taken below decks on the '*De Wadden*' schooner next to the '*Lusitania*' propeller to see the Blackbirds' nests, three or four old ones on various girders and portholes! No sign of the Grey Wagtails. The suspicion was that they had been driven away to nest elsewhere by Pied Wagtails.

CENTRAL PARK, Wallasey: Swallows back at traditional nesting site in old 'farm buildings' – two miles from Pier Head – probably the nearest to the city centre. Whinchat at Bidston Dock pool.

Here, up in those blue suburban skies……

6 MAY: SWIFTS OVER PENNY LANE…Thank you for sending such an 'exclusive' birthday card. As I've lived in this area for 53 years I can remember Penny Lane looking as uncluttered as in your sketch! The usual three Swifts arrived 6-7 May – always three to start with, more later.   Margaret Thompson.

Margaret had already written saying that 'her' Swifts always arrived on her birthday in May and I just happened to have drawn a picture of Swifts over Penny Lane - to make a pun on the line from the song – 'here, beneath those blue suburban skies'!

…AND IN HUYTON: One of my favourite things is the arrival of the Swifts in May. For me one of the best events of the year is to be in the back garden in the early evening with a nice glass of wine watching the Swifts screaming through the air and returning to their nests. To me this tells you that summer really has arrived. Must sign off now: got to catch the off-licence.   Tony Craven

CUCKOOS AND COLLARED DOVES: Tony also reported his only Cuckoo of the spring – on 8 May at Formby – around the same time as I heard my only Cuckoo on Bidston Moss; mutual confirmation that this was the peak time for Cuckoos passing through the area, but now very much a rarity compared with 30-40 years ago when most people still heard the Cuckoo in spring. 30-40 years ago we did not have Collared Doves in this part of the world – first nesting record at the Mariners' Homes in Egremont, Wallasey, in 1961 – which are now often mistaken for Cuckoos because of their 'coo-coo, coo' calls. I had personal confirmation of this confusion when I overheard a lady at a bus stop saying she was woken every morning by a Cuckoo which I knew to be a Collared Dove.

38

SUNDAY 6 MAY : PIER HEAD TO PARADISE (STREET) NATURE TRAIL

A vision of reconstructed Castle Walls on Chavasse Park

It was time to invite BBC Radio Merseyside listeners to come and see some of the things I had found around the Pier Head, Albert Dock and Chavasse Park on my Friday morning visits. We met at the Pier Head where the Herring Gull immediately obliged by taking more nest material up to the nest it was building on a chimney of the Port of Liverpool Building. Even better, as I was describing the Blackbirds' nests I had been shown in the *'De Wadden'* schooner, a male Blackbird arrived and flew in through the bow porthole to feed young inside. Three male Mallard flew past, a number that had been seen on several occasions increasing suspicions that they were nesting somewhere close.

We saw what an easy life the immature gulls had around the Pier Head. When they were hungry they simply had to fly down into Canning Dock and pull a mussel off the dock wall. Not quite so easy though, because they had to be broken open and usually a brother, sister, relative or friend was waiting ready to steal it!

We were also able to confirm that the Goldfinch's nest by the Yellow Submarine had either been rebuilt or replaced and was in use again. We also inspected the Mistle Thrush nests around Chavasse Park – two built by the same pair by the fire station, one at the top of the tall lamp-post in the car park and one which was in probably the smallest tree in the whole area - cleverly disguised in a clump of dead leaves!

I had found a beautiful female Emperor Moth that morning which I couldn't resist bringing to show the group (releasing it again later, of course) and I was able to tell listeners about my vision of recreating Liverpool's Castle Walls on Chavasse Park (with moat) as an added tourist attraction but more important to ensure that the area remained open space.

The group seemed impressed and fascinated by just how much 'nature' there was and how much was going on in this famous part of the city.

SUNDAY 13 MAY: STANLEY PARK

FA CUP FINAL CELEBRATION WALK

Venmore Street. The Kop in spring

I had to anticipate Liverpool's victory to announce this walk on the Friday before the cup final was being played! Liverpool 2 Arsenal 1. Liverpool had only got there by knocking out Tranmere in the quarter-finals. And I suppose we could argue that we were also celebrating Everton's survival in the Premier Division, recently confirmed!

We met outside the Kop and walked round into Stanley Park where we were greeted by the vigorous song of a Song Thrush – also celebrating, it seemed! Later we had excellent views of Blackcap (first time for some), Blackbird and Chaffinch singing close together all at the same time. A Blue Tit was feeding young in a nest in the monument by the bridge over the recently refurbished lake where a Coot had built a nest on a tiny wooden platform and Mute Swans were planning to nest on the island (thwarted by vandals, I heard later in the year).

We saw a couple of Holly Blue butterflies (no Reds?) around the many big old holly trees which were showing their tiny flowers, not often noticed. The best picture of the day was probably the five baby Long Tailed Tits just out of the nest huddled together amongst cherry blossom waiting to be fed by busy parents.

The general conclusion was: who needs football when you can have all this – for nothing – just round the corner! However, the Nature Watch football connection was to continue for a few weeks to come.

RUDDY DUCKS AT WEST KIRBY AND BIDSTON MOSS: On my way to Stanley Park I had seen a male Ruddy Duck on the pools by Bidston Station where one had also been seen a couple of times the year before. This American duck has been spreading very rapidly since escaping from collections and was already nesting on the Cheshire Meres by 1985. One has also been reported at Gilroy Road Pond in West Kirby.   Mick and Betty Griffiths

STONEYCROFT: A warm, sunny weekend. Coal Tits spent the afternoon sunning themselves with outspread wings on the branch of a conifer. Peacock butterflies were flying.   Margaret Parry

15 MAY: NATURE WATCH NEWS

By 15 May all trees were in full leaf at last. Lilac, laburnum and chestnut were in flower, hawthorn still only just starting – all about two weeks later than last year. The beautiful displays of berberis were finishing but there were still no roses compared with a first on 3 May last year. Bluebells were at their peak, Cowslips already past their best, but many more wild flowers had appeared: the first tall white Cow Parsley, purple Common Vetch and yellow Bird's Foot Trefoil: lots of pink Herb Robert along with Red Campions. Buttercups joining dandelions in grassy areas.

The Small Tortoiseshell butterflies and Peacocks which had come out of hibernation were already starting to die off to be followed by a new generation later. Still only the one Comma – back on 10 April – but Whites and Speckled Woods were now very numerous. A Speckled Wood had even found its way to the tiny 'oasis' of St Nicholas churchyard at the Pier Head! After a first Holly Blue on 16 April and another on 30 April they were reported from both sides of the Mersey from 10 May when holly bushes and trees were showing a lot of their tiny flowers. Common Blues should also be appearing now, out on open grassland. No Small Coppers as yet. Has anybody seen them? On 6 May I found a beautiful female Emperor Moth (should be called Empress?!) – bigger than any butterfly, alive and well on the platform at Bidston Station! More craneflies, ladybirds, wasps – and ants of course!

Migrating Little Gulls have stayed at Crosby Marina and Seaforth well into May in record numbers peaking at over 800. Blue Tits have been seen feeding young in nest-boxes but there have been many reports of 'problems' this year. Hopefully a clearer picture later. I saw first young Long Tailed Tits out of the nest on 9 May, the same day as first young Robins and Hedge Sparrows flew the nest. Plenty of well-grown, independent young Blackbirds this year. Mistle Thrushes sitting on second (or even third?) broods, males singing in thundery rain.

All summer migrants have arrived by now and I've been very excited to find a definite Garden Warbler this year – much scarcer and more elusive than the name suggests! Is the Garden Warbler being squeezed out by Blackcaps which have increased and expanded in most parks and garden areas many also staying here for the winter and not leaving the Garden Warbler much of a chance?

After first Swifts on 29 April the big influx of local birds came from 12 May onwards. Grasshopper Warbler reported at Childwall Fields and one has been singing at Bidston Moss since 25 April where a Cuckoo was calling at first light on 7 May. Swallows have returned to Central Park, Wallasey, probably the Swallows nesting closest to the Pier Head two miles away.

8 MAY: RIVER MERSEY: A Kittiwake followed the ferry again from Seacombe to Woodside where the male Peregrine was seen on the ventilation shaft for about ten minutes before it flew off and disappeared over Hamilton Square.

POULTON, Wallasey: House Martins were busy at traditional nesting sites on houses around Poulton Primary School.

SUNDAY 20 MAY: WIRRAL COASTAL WALK

LIVERPOOL CUP TREBLE CELEBRATIONS

The Strand at 16.00 on 20 May 2001

The original plan had been to meet at Woodside and walk across to Seacombe whilst everybody else was doing the charity walk from Seacombe round to Thurstaston. But we had such good views of the Peregrines and so much to talk about we never got further than Woodside Ferry! At one point the male Peregrine returned to the ventilation shaft with prey which it plucked for about 10-15 minutes. Apparently this was too long for the female Peregrine who flew down from the nest on the station tower, collected the meal and then flew back to the nest site. She hopped down out of sight but flying feathers confirmed she could only be feeding young which may have just hatched that very day.

The group was happy to take my word for it that Lapwings and Skylarks were nesting on the Twelve Quays site just along the way and seemed to be in a hurry to get the ferry back to the Pier Head. Since the FA Cup Nature Watch in Stanley Park Liverpool had clinched an historic treble by winning the UEFA as well as the Worthington and FA Cups. The team and cups were being paraded around the city bringing some half a million people onto the streets. Most of them seemed to be in the Strand and Chavasse Park (a big turn-out on our Pier Head to Paradise –Street- Nature Trail!). Trophy-shaped balloons were going up everywhere and at 15.20 as I waited in the middle of the Strand a Peregrine glided slowly along towards the Liver Buildings apparently mesmerised by the balloons wondering whether they were worth attacking or not. People had climbed all over the Yellow Submarine and up into the trees. Poor Goldfinches nesting there, I thought, but they do have red faces so are presumably Liverpool supporters themselves!

22 MAY: ABERCROMBY SQUARE: My office is on the bridge that spans Oxford Street joining the physics building to Senate House. There is a Mistle Thrush nesting on the window ledge near my desk. We have covered the window and made a spy-hole for optimum viewing hoping that she will soon be feeding young.

K.W.Williams

42

23 MAY: SCHOOL NATURE WATCH, the Breck, Wallasey: Now that many young birds had flown the nest I took a group from Poulton Primary School along to the Breck where they were able to view the empty nests of Mistle Thrush, Blackbird, Wren, Hedge Sparrow, Collared Dove, Carrion Crow and Long Tailed Tit. We found a Song Thrush 'anvil' with lots of broken snail shells. An Orange-Tip butterfly was flying along Breck Road. It was easy to see that even in this technological age young children are still fascinated by the wonder of nature and the natural world around us. But somebody has to take them out and show them. Their teachers agreed whole-heartedly. 'But there is no time for such things in the national curriculum'. Something wrong with the curriculum, perhaps?

I remember when I was at school, 65 years ago, there was a nature table in the corner of the classroom where we put leaves or acorns which we had collected on the way to school. Muriel Hammond, Garston

TWELVE QUAYS: An interesting collection of wild flowers (no, not weeds!) growing along Shore Road towards Morpeth Dock. A Lapwing was diving and calling over the open land by the river while two Skylarks were singing overhead. Linnets and Whitethroat by the One O'Clock Gun on the waterfront – all just across the river from the Pier Head.

24 MAY: RAVENS AND OTTERS IN CHESTER: Ravens have been nesting on Chester Cathedral for six years now. As far as I know Chester was the first case of Ravens nesting on a cathedral or any other building for that matter, though they will nest on high pylons. It seems logical to assume that birds had wandered here from North Wales and that the birds which had turned up at the Anglican Cathedral in Liverpool were descendants of the Chester Ravens who were simply moving 'from home to home'. The young had now flown but the bulky nest on the east side of the cathedral tower was an impressive reminder of one of the more spectacular developments in the region.

Later in the year reports came in that Otters had bred in Cheshire for the first time in 40 years. The official Otter Poo Sniffer had also found 'concrete' evidence of Otters on the Dee at Chester.

26 MAY: LOGGERHEADS, North Wales: On a walk along the Leete Valley we found about 30 species of flowers and ferns growing on the limestone which are generally absent from the sandstone which is characteristic of Merseyside proper. Of special interest: Toothwort, Herb Paris, Twayblade, Early Purple Orchid, Agrimony, Rock Rose, Spindle Tree, Greater Celandine, Wild Arum, Crosswort, Salad Burnet, Goldilocks, Sanicle, Woodruff. To the general public, however, the most impressive botanical sight – and smell!- of the Leete Valley are the huge beds of Ramsons or Wild Garlic which follow the river the whole length of its course almost illuminating the shady valley like a mass of white candles. The woods were remarkably quiet. No sign of Pied Flycatchers or Wood Warbler, two of the specialities here, and no Dipper as hoped. Two Buzzards circling together and Great Spotted Woodpecker and Blackcap song were the only noticeable birds. Peacock and Orange-Tip also seen.

SUNDAY 27 MAY: THE LIVERPOOL OPEN
ALLERTON GOLF COURSE CALDERSTONES PARK

The Liverpool Open had been held the day before in aid of the BBC Radio Merseyside Charitable Trust so there was only one place to go in the hope of seeing birdies, eagles, perhaps even albatross?! We met at the Coach House in Calderstones Park and walked down towards the lake where BBC Radio Merseyside had also inaugurated its first Bluebell Field of Celebration.

Swallows and Pied Wagtails were obviously nesting around the Coach House. Sparrowhawks, Tawny Owls and foxes are also in the park though we saw none of them during our visit. We were told about the almost albino Magpie which had been reported by many people in the Calderstones area. Wilma from Woolton was able to tell us that it was born in a nest by Newborough School two years earlier and is seen most often in the Menlove Avenue area. Kenny from Gateacre and Tony from Crosby had also seen it.

A pair of Canada Geese had five young and there were also young Mallard and Moorhens on the lake. We had good views of a Great Spotted Woodpecker flying and heard a Nuthatch piping above our heads.

But the natural wonder of Calderstones Park has to be the Allerton Oak (not the name of a pub as somebody at BBC Radio Merseyside seemed to think!). This is what Friends of Childwall Woods and Fields wrote about it in one of their newsletters:

There are few of us who do not know the old Allerton Oak in Calderstones Park. As children – along with stories of Robin Hood – we were told that the tree was 1000 years old and that the Witan, the Anglo-Saxon council of wise men, used to meet under its branches. Hardly true, we now realise, but it was the stuff that fired up the imagination for 'make-believe' games during many happy summer holidays.

The wonderful thing is: seedlings from this tree are now growing in Childwall Fields. Trees of Time and Place in the Mersey Forest recently organised children from Childwall Church of England Primary School to plant them. We hope these will last, shall we say, another 1000 years, so that the folklore associated with their parent will live on.

We were also shown the Pocket Handkerchief Tree, still in flower with lots of 'paper handkerchief' petals hanging down from its 'upside down' magnolia-like flowers. A walk along the path by the golf course did not produce anything of special interest: not an eagle in sight!

27 MAY: This was also the day when I noticed first roses in flower – about two weeks later than usual. Also first Bramble flowers and Broad-Leaved Willowherb along Canning Dock with lots of Hop Trefoil. First Meadow Cranesbill and first Common Blue butterfly of the year on Kidney Vetch sheltering from a shower of rain.

30 MAY: BIDSTON HILL: Two Great Spotted Woodpecker nests easily located because of the noisy young inside! Bullfinches by Tam O'Shanter Urban Farm. Foxglove and Goatsbeard in flower.

31 MAY : NATURE WATCH NEWS

The weather stayed kind for most of May this year and we had some really wonderful days as gardens started filling with colour and more wild flowers appeared. Rhododendrons were now at their best and first roses at last, two or three weeks later than last year. By the end of the month the hawthorn was looking glorious white with more white in banks of tall Cow Parsley along lanes and hedgerows, Ox-eye Daisies, first Guelder Rose, Elderberry and Bramble flowers. Lots of yellow Broom taking over from the gorse now fading; more yellow as buttercups, hawkweeds and Goatsbeard – like giant dandelions – appear on grassland. Plenty of Bird's Foot Trefoil and Hop Clover – also yellow – and Red Campions, Red Clover, Common Vetch and in shady places Herb Robert adding pink and purple to the tapestry of colour.

On 26 May I was shown about 30 species of flowers on the limestone of the Leet Valley, Loggerheads, North Wales, which are not usually found on the sandstone and clay of Merseyside proper, including Herb Paris and Twayblade.

The only report of Brimstone butterfly so far came from the Chester area on 24 May. By the end of May any Small Tortoiseshells or Peacocks still flying were looking tired and worn. Look out for their caterpillars on nettles through June. Whites were now most noticeable and abundant and Orange-Tips were still flying. More Holly Blues were seen in the second half of May. Common Blues and Small Copper reported from 27 May, Small Heath and Large Skipper (both about the same size!) on 31 May. That makes 13 species for the year so far, just about as many as can be expected in this part of the country but with more to follow. Big Meadow Browns will be appearing in the next week or two and look out for migrant Red Admirals, even Painted Ladies and possibly Clouded Yellows as last year. By the end of May the first beautiful turquoise damselflies were flying and first dragonflies had been seen.

Young Starlings and sparrows were out of the nest around 17 May turning gardens into noisy nurseries. On 18 May I watched a Lesser Blackbacked Gull collecting nest material in Chavasse Park, first hand confirmation that both Herring Gulls and Lesser Blackbacks are nesting on city centre buildings. A young Tawny Owl was rescued from a vicious attack by Crows and Magpies in Childwall Woods.

While most birds are busy nesting, butterflies and orchids will take centre stage in June. Bee Orchids have been spreading 'like wildfire' along motorways, grass verges, car parks etc. So please check 'everywhere' so that we can put a detailed picture together. They should be out any time now.

MAY FLOWERS: Bird's Foot Trefoil, Kidney Vetch, Common Vetch, Bush Vetch, Hairy Tare, Herb Robert, Scarlet Pimpernel, Water Cress, Penny Cress, White Campion, Stitchwort, Clovers, Burnet Rose, Cow Parsley, Bramble, Goosegrass, Sowthistle, Oxford Ragwort, Yellow Flag, Silverweed, Ragged Robin, Wild Pansy, Columbine.

We walked up from Bidston Station through the village where plenty of sparrows were chirruping. Swallows were dashing round farm buildings and low over grass. We saw Goatsbeard and Foxglove in flower – and a first black and red Cinnabar Moth - before turning into the woods where I sent young William ahead in search of the woodpecker's nest. He soon pointed to the tree where the noise was coming from and it was not long before we all had good views of the parents coming to feed them. Strange calls further along sounded rather like Pied Flycatcher – which have nested here in the past – but we weren't able to confirm it.

Past another Great Spotted Woodpecker's nest in a pine tree this time to Tam O'Shanter urban farm now open again after the height of the foot and mouth scare.

The farm is always worth a visit – if only to see children clearly enjoying themselves in a simple, natural environment – no thought of computers or TV here!

We walked back past the windmill, observatory and lighthouse enjoying the magnificent views. Of all the hills and mountains I've climbed all over Europe Bidston Hill remains unique and is seriously underestimated by many people on Merseyside who simply take it for granted. As Greenwich is to the world for time, so Bidston Hill for tides.

Together with the birds we had seen around Bidston Station we had a total of 43 species for the day – a new Sunday Nature Watch record which remained unbeaten for the rest of the year showing just how important this area is for local wildlife as well as local history.

4 JUNE: BIDSTON MOSS: A busy day for butterflies: Speckled Woods, Large Skipper (first seen on 31 May), a fresh Small Tortoiseshell, Small Copper, 3 Small Heaths (also reported from the North Wirral coast). It was around this time that most listeners reported young Blue Tits leaving nest-boxes – later than last year.

5 JUNE: BEE ORCHIDS – A BOTANICAL SENSATION ON MERSEYSIDE

My wildflower book (1970 edition) describes the Bee Orchid as " a rather rare plant of chalky soils, more often in the south than in the north". This does not exactly sound like Merseyside! Yet in the last 15 years or so Bee Orchids have started turning up in all sorts of unexpected places. Experts will tell you that they will grow where the soil has been disturbed. But there has always been plenty of building, destruction and disturbed soil on Merseyside – for hundreds of years - without Bee Orchids ever being seen. Other factors must be at work, new factors, and I suspect that traffic fumes, even artificial lighting, may play a part in this mystery.

Results of my survey in 2000 were reported on BBC Radio Merseyside. I counted a total of about 850 in the Bidston Moss area, one of the first places they were found – around 1985. But the fascination of the Bee Orchids for me is more to do with their simple, elegant beauty than rarity or sensation.

The white buds were visible amongst grasses by the beginning of June and by 5 June the first pink petals and brown 'boots' were showing. It would be interesting to see – with the help of BBC Radio Merseyside listeners – just how far they had penetrated into the city centre.

Marsh Orchids have always been native to Merseyside and they were also starting to show their first purple flowers.

YOUNG PEREGRINES AT HAMILTON SQUARE AND STANLEY DOCK: It was on 5 June that I first noticed at least two downy white Peregrine chicks at the nest site at Hamilton Square Station and I received news that the pair at Stanley Dock tobacco warehouse had also successfully hatched young again.

AND GREY WAGTAILS - ANOTHER MERSEYSIDE SPECIALITY: Later the same day I came across an adult Grey Wagtail with a young bird – by the lake in Birkenhead Park, the first young seen in 2001. They may have nested in or near the park itself but they could have moved here from a more remote and secure nesting site somewhere in the docks not too far away. I also found two more Great Spotted Woodpecker nests – again by the noise coming from them. I measured the nests at only 1.8642 miles from the Pier Head – in other words 3 km!

6 JUNE: GEESE OVER WAVERTREE: On the way to Dad's I stopped and stared at about 20 geese in V-formation flying from north to south. Local housepainters have now decided I'm peculiar!   Margaret Thompson

Don't worry, Margaret! This is an occupational hazard for urban Nature Watchers! And in fact a very interesting observation: no doubt Canada Geese moving to the Mersey at Frodsham Score where large numbers (1000+) spend a month of flightless moult at this time of the year.

8 JUNE: HAMILTON SQUARE: One Peregrine chick already scratching out white down as it gained real feathers.

SUNDAY 10 JUNE: MERSEY RIVER FESTIVAL

Narrowboats in Albert Dock.

A hundred narrowboats, the tall ships *'Earl of Pembroke'*, *' Phoenix'* and *'HMS Ramsey'* had all come into Albert Dock for the annual celebrations. We met outside BBC Radio Merseyside in Paradise Street and walked across Chavasse Park where we noticed a lot of cottony cushion scale – now infesting trees all over Merseyside. It is a small beetle which came into this country in the 1960s and has now reached the North of England. We also saw that the Goldfinch's nest by the Yellow Submarine had been dislodged and was now literally hanging by a thread – no doubt during the football celebrations on 20 May. We optimistically 'assumed' that the young had already flown.

We had a look at our very own 'Botany Bay' – the interesting variety of flowers growing between the cobbles by Canning Dock, including Viola tricolor – Wild Pansy – Penny Cress, Common Vetch, Tufted Vetch and Prickly Lettuce, but security prevented us from viewing the 'coral reef' growing on the landing stage in Salthouse Dock (sea anemones etc.).

Then we took the ferry across to Woodside – good views of one of the young Peregrines – and were back on the river just in time for the Parade of Sail. Later the Peregrines had serious competition from a 'Battle of Britain' fly-past by a Lancaster Bomber and a Spitfire!

11 JUNE: BIDSTON MOSS: Confirmation that Dabchicks had young at the pools by Bidston Station, almost certainly the nearest to the Pier Head just 3 miles away.

GARSTON: I counted a total of 32 frogs at my pond this year but probably more. Most of the spawn seems to have survived and I've a couple of hundred tadpoles at least.   Kathy Andrews

13 JUNE: BEE ORCHIDS – IN LEEDS STREET! I had been keen to find out how close the Bee Orchids had penetrated to the city centre so I set out from BBC Radio Merseyside heading 'north' via Moorfields and the car parks at old Exchange Station which looked quite promising. None there but when I crossed Leeds Street I found a small strip of good-looking grass right on top of the entrance to the railway tunnel into Moorfields. From a distance I could already see the purple of about 30 Marsh Orchids and then, yes, two Bee Orchids – here only about half a mile from the Pier Head! Also Common Blue butterfly and Cinnabar Moth.

15 JUNE: NATURE WATCH NEWS

As promised in the last Nature Watch News the first Bee Orchids were seen in flower on 5 June, Marsh Orchids a few days earlier. Bee Orchids were virtually unknown on Merseyside until about 1985 when a colony of 130 was discovered near Bidston Station. Last year Bee Orchids were reported from all over Merseyside and this year I was keen to see how far they had penetrated into the city centre. On 13 June I was delighted to find two Bee Orchids right on top of the Moorfields train tunnel entrance by Leeds Street along with about 30 Marsh Orchids, Common Blue butterflies, Cinnabar Moth, a singing Whitethroat and rabbits! All this just half a mile from the Liver Buildings at the Pier Head! Please check all 'wasteland' and grassland for both Bee Orchids and Marsh Orchids and enjoy these majestic flowers while they last. The Bee Orchids will be finished in two or three weeks, the Marsh Orchids will last longer, probably right through July.

There is a whole colony of Herring Gulls and Lesser Blackbacks nesting on the roof of the Bestway Cash and Carry at the Wallasey Tunnel entrance. Swans, Lapwings and probably Skylarks nested on the site of the old Clarence Dock 'Three Ugly Sisters' power station where Grey Wagtails were seen feeding young in a nest.

Also a suspicion that Shelducks and Canada Geese may have nested there as well as the Peregrines on the Stanley Dock tobacco warehouse. All within a mile of the Pier Head so we really are turning the city centre, river and docklands into Britain's first and best Metropolitan Wildlife Park!

We have received reports of Ravens nesting 200 feet up on a gasholder in St Helens, quite possibly the birds which abandoned the Anglican Cathedral earlier in the year. Ravens, Peregrines, Buzzards in Knowsley and Wirral: perhaps we should start expecting Red Kites next!

No reports of migrant butterflies as yet but a warm southerly wind on 14 June felt favourable. Only one Small Tortoiseshell reported since 2 June but a new generation should be appearing any time now, also first Meadow Browns. Cinnabar Moths have been seen since 2 June with the similarly black and red Burnet Moths ready to hatch from their cocoons in the coming days.

HUYTON: A couple of weeks ago I heard an almighty commotion going on in the back garden. Expecting to see a cat I was amazed to spot through the shrubs the unmistakable charcoal and grey barred breast of a beautiful female Sparrowhawk. I held her gaze for about five seconds, then she took off with a lifeless fledgling grasped in her talons. She went straight up to an incredible height with a lone Blackbird vainly giving chase. I actually felt privileged for this bird to come into our garden. I think you will understand what I mean.

Tony Craven

15 JUNE: LUCKY RAVENS LAND ON ST HELENS GAS HOLDER: This is what the Transco press release said:

A pair of Ravens and their chicks have been spotted nesting 200ft up a Transco gas holder at Jackson Street in St Helens.

In recent times the birds have begun returning to more urban areas. They are becoming more common in the North West and have been spotted times at Chester Cathedral and the Anglican Cathedral in Liverpool.

Far from being seen as the evil scavengers they were in the past Ravens are now believed to bring good luck. Legend has it that they nest on top of the Tower of London and should they ever leave it will signal the end of the monarchy!

Phil O'Sullivan Transco Networks Operations Manager said:*" We have a pair of Peregrine Falcons already using the holder roof as a place to tear up and eat their prey. It is nice to see these rare birds returning to such a built up area and using our holder as a safe place to nest and feed. Let's hope they bring good luck to the people of St Helens!"*

15 JUNE: BEE ORCHIDS – IN OLD HALL STREET! I had arranged to go with a Daily Post photographer to take pictures of the Bee Orchids I had found in Leeds Street on 13 June. Before I went in I had a quick look around the car park just over the road in Brook Street and found another two Bee Orchids there – only a stone's throw from the Liver Buildings at the centre of our BBC Radio Merseyside Nature Watch survey!

16 JUNE: MARSH ORCHIDS – IN PARADISE STREET! The climax of this year's orchid search was a find of about 30 Marsh Orchids growing on the site of the old Sailors' Home on the corner of Paradise Street and Canning Place – visible from reception at BBC Radio Merseyside! You can't bring nature much closer than that!

BALLOONS IN BIRKENHEAD PARK: Another annual event on Merseyside is the 'Balloons Across The Mersey' festival when hot air balloons set off from Birkenhead Park to cross the Mersey to the Liverpool side. But because of the foot and mouth outbreak the balloons remained tethered in the park with an impressive music and light show that evening.

SEFTON PARK: Just a few notes about unusual sightings. A Great Spotted Woodpecker and a Nuthatch have been seen sharing the same tree. The two nests are less than two feet apart on opposite sides of the tree. Both with young (fledged 13-14 June). Foxes are around the Dell and Grey Squirrel near Lark Lane. A Buzzard was flying over on 12 June. Terrapins, quite large, can be seen basking on logs round the small island at the far end of the bandstand lake. A Kingfisher around the end of May.

Alan McGlynn

BOOTLE CANAL UPDATE: On our canal bank we now have ducklings, Coot chicks, Moorhen, sparrows, Starlings, tits, thrush (Mistle?) and Blackbird.

Kevin McNulty

50

The joy of finding Bee Orchids in Brook Street...

...and Marsh Orchids in Leeds Street (below)

51

Marsh Orchids
– Canning Place

**SUNDAY 17
JUNE:
CITY
SAFARI:
OLD HALL
STREET-
STANLEY
DOCK**

*Stanley Dock
tobacco
warehouse*

We met outside the Daily Post and Echo offices in Old Hall Street to see the Bee Orchids there and in Leeds Street where we also saw rabbits in Lanyork Road, a Whitehroat singing and Common Blue butterflies flying again. We carried on to the canal at the Eldonian Village where we were greeted by Steve (Burke) who had been on an earlier Nature Watch and his mum Vera who told us how she had been frightened out of her wits by a huge Heron which had suddenly flown up out of their canal side garden one morning. Round the corner there was quite a crowd at the lock gates which were just being opened to let the narrow boats through which had been stuck in Albert Dock since the River Festival a week earlier because of the wind and tides. Robert who works for British Waterways on the canal was able to tell us that he often sees Kingfishers on the canal out of the breeding season; Cormorants, Tufted Ducks and Great Crested Grebes on the canal in winter. While we were talking the Stanley Dock Peregrines were circling over our heads apparently trying to coax the young to take first flights. We found Grey Wagtails nesting at Clarence Dock graving dock where Terry on security told me Mute Swans had nested with 5 young and about 8 Lapwings and Skylarks had been on the site during the breeding season, obviously nesting there.

To round the day off we ended up back on the ferry. The Kittiwake which had been seen several times already showed up again and we found one young Peregrine up on the tower at Hamilton Square Station. In the end we felt we had been to some far away place for the day, yet everything we had seen was within sight of the Pier Head never more than a mile away!

CENTRAL PARK, Wallasey: Two young Grey Wagtails, probably young from the nest in the back yard in Liscard shopping centre.

WAVERLEY PADDLE STEAMER IN LIVERPOOL

Photo:George Muskett, Maghull

19 JUNE: We went on the 'Waverley' to Anglesey – a bit misty but we did see some seals off Anglesey when the mist cleared.   Edmund and Irene Jelley – West Kirby

20 JUNE: We went on the Waverley trip to the Blackpool coast. It was great to see Gannets diving with Crosby in the background!

Visitors to BBC Radio Merseyside at the Wirral Show

GARSTON UPDATE: My baby frogs have started to emerge from the pond – perfect miniatures!   Kathy Andrews

BIDSTON MOSS: First Meadow Brown butterfly of the year. Speckled Wood, Small Copper, Large Skipper, Small Heath, Small Tortoiseshell, Common Blue: with the Whites, nine species of butterflies now flying. Seaforth-Hightown is the only area where Wall Browns have been reported, though they are also included in the list of butterflies seen at Childwall Woods and Fields. Bee Orchids probably at their peak now. First Rosebay Willowherb in flower. Nursery Web Spider 'tents' in the grass.

21 JUNE: MIDSUMMER'S DAY: Graham and Carl who both work at Hamilton Square told me independently that they had seen four Peregrines on the station tower.

22 JUNE: PIER HEAD TO PARADISE (STREET) NATURE TRAIL: There is a small patch of 'wasteland' next to the Baltic Fleet along Wapping which turned out to be a veritable wildlife oasis. At least six Common Blues were flying, attracted by the Hop Clover that was growing there in abundance, also Red and White Clover.

FERRY CROSS THE MERSEY: Except for the big gulls nesting in the city centre the river is very quiet at this time of the year. The Blackheaded and Common Gulls which come to the Mersey in their thousands for the winter are all away at their nesting grounds. Only one Blackheaded and one immature Common Gull seen from the ferry and no Kittiwake on this occasion.

*The
ventilation
shaft,
Woodside
Ferry*

PEREGRINE TRAGEDY AT HAMILTON SQUARE: David Connolly who works in the restaurant at Woodside Ferry told me the Peregrines had been very noisy and excited around the ventilation shaft that morning at about 7.30. I took this to be a sign that the young were now having first flying lessons but there was bad news to come.

That evening one of the young Peregrines fell from the station tower and was crushed under the wheels of a passing bus. The following Tuesday (26 June) another Peregrine was retrieved from inside the ventilation shaft. It was very weak and dirty and had obviously been there for some time – possibly explaining the excitement David had noticed - four days earlier. The Peregrine was taken to the Wildlife Centre at Thurstaston where it was being looked after by wildlife officer Malcolm Ingham.

22 JUNE: RAVENS – ON GASHOLDER IN SOUTHPORT! The photo which I received looked just like the one I had been sent from St Helens (15 June) – only the names had been changed..! Transco told me that they had 87 such gasholders in the NW – plenty of room for more Ravens in the future!

MERSEY SHORE: GARSTON DOCKS TO HALE LIGHTHOUSE: From early in the year you are surrounded by the sound of Skylarks, with Lapwings skilfully twisting and turning in flight. Partridge in the surrounding fields. Down on the Mersey shore there were Dunlin, Oystercatcher, Redshank, Ringed Plover, Shelduck, Teal. Early spring brought Chiffchaff, Willow Warbler, Whitethroat, Sedge Warbler and Grasshopper Warbler. One day I 'froze' as I caught sight of a Weasel amongst the brambles. Using a trick I had learnt from a friend I pursed my lips and made a loud kissing noise. Sure enough, the Weasel instantly headed towards me up to about 15 feet away. What a great feeling that encounter left me with. There is a small colony of Sand Martins nesting below the old airport. Tony Craven

It was special in many ways: the biggest turn out of the year – both people and wildlife! And a beautiful, fine, warm day. Bidston Moss is special to Merseyside as it is the nearest large expanse of natural – or at least semi-natural –open land to the Pier Head at the heart of the Merseyside region only 2-3 miles away across the river. In an article in the summer edition of the Wirral Journal I described the pool at the end of Bidston Dock as Wirral's secret wildlife haven. Just on 100 species of birds were recorded on Bidston Moss in 2000, including Great Crested Grebe, Dabchick, Water Rail, Common and Green Sandpiper, Partridge and Lapwing both nesting, Barn Owl, Short Eared Owl, Buzzard. Not only birds, of course: flowers and butterflies, foxes and fishing – including our very own DOCKLANDS LOCH NESS MONSTER – probably a giant eel which people claim to see in the pool at Bidston Dock.

After looking at Bee Orchids and Marsh Orchids we found Common Spotted Orchids, dragonflies and damselflies, Burnet Moth caterpillars, cocoons and flying adults, lots of baby frogs, a family of newts under a plank, a headless gull by the fox's den, baby Wolf Spiders in a 'tent' protected by a very aggressive mother, ants tending a herd of blackfly on Guelder Rose, a carp in the water weed on the Birket, a pellet and bird feathers on the Kestrel's favourite feeding stone, Whitethroats feeding young in a nest in brambles, Swallows feeding young on the wires, seven species of butterflies, 42 species of birds. A very special day indeed!

26 JUNE: NORTH WIRRAL COAST: Five Pyramidal Orchids were in the same place as last year with another 'feeble' specimen close by. A lot of Small Heath butterflies, also Common Blues and Small Skippers (first seen 22 June). First migrant Red Admirals: at least five overtook me heading NE along the coast.

29 JUNE: First lavetera flowers, a type of tree mallow which seems to be increasing in popularity – especially with Bumble Bees. Vapourer Moth caterpillars – like tiny painted Chinese dragons – hatching from eggs on the outside of female's cocoon.

30 JUNE NATURE WATCH NEWS

After Bee Orchids next to the Daily Post offices on 15 June, the very next day I found about 30 Marsh Orchids right here in Paradise Street about 100 yards from the BBC Radio Merseyside studios! A pair of Common Blue butterflies in Chavasse Park and another six by the Baltic Fleet. It was also on 16 June that I found a first Burnet Moth cocoon which I took into the studio on 22 June and again on 29 June after it had hatched and flown – before and after, so to speak! Cinnabar Moths, also black and red, will be dying off soon, but look out for their black and orange striped caterpillars on Ragwort.

The first Meadow Brown was reported on 20 June and they should now remain abundant into September. Gatekeepers should be appearing any time now. No reports of Wall Browns sent in, but I hear that about 30 were counted at Seaforth Nature Reserve. Look out for their second generation in July - August. 26 June was a glorious day with a strong, warm SE breeze. A few Red Admirals were seen on local coasts, no Painted Ladies or Clouded Yellows as yet. Green-Veined Whites also reported which makes 17 species of butterflies on Merseyside so far this year.

Another pair of Ravens has been reported nesting on a gasholder – this time in Southport. Transco tell me that they have 87 such gasholders in the NW of England, plenty of room for more Ravens, so watch this space….!

The story of the Peregrines at Hamilton Square Station took a dramatic turn this last week. I have been assured that four young birds have been seen on the station tower, though I have only ever seen one at a time. On 22 June one of the young birds fell from the tower and was crushed under the wheels of a bus. Then on 26 June another bird was found in the tunnel ventilation shaft. It was rescued and taken to Thurstaston Wildlife Centre to be rested and cleaned up. Hopefully more good news later.

Listeners have reported Buzzards over Storeton and Little Sutton, more or less confirming that they are nesting in mid-Wirral again. A pair of Blackbirds in a Hoylake garden had their nest raided twice – by Grey Squirrels. Young Grey Wagtails have been seen in both Birkenhead Park and Central Park, Wallasey, also on the shore at New Ferry. A family of Shelduck at Caldy and I saw a family with ten ducklings bobbing along on the Mersey at Bromborough Dock. Reliable reports of a Nightingale singing in Garswood, St Helens in April and a Corncrake calling there in June. A Kittiwake has stayed on the river all summer, usually seen between Seacombe and Woodside. Blackheaded Gulls have started to return from their nesting colonies, soon to be joined by Common Gulls. In Sefton Park Great Spotted Woodpecker and Nuthatch shared the same tree with nesting holes only about two feet apart! Small numbers of Oystercatchers, Redshank, Curlew and Dunlin back on local beaches.

**SUNDAY 1 JULY
THE SEABIRD
COLONY – IN SCOTTY
ROAD!**

It was clear that many Herring Gulls and Lesserblackbacks were nesting up on city centre rooftops but the nests were not visible from ground level. On 13 June I had discovered a small colony on the relatively flat and low roof of the Bestway Cash and Carry at the entrance to the Wallasey Tunnel in Scotland Road. Here you could look down onto the nests from the other side of the main road from the hill by Burlington Street.

We met on the steps of Liverpool Museum to walk up to the colony but before we had even set off gulls were in the sky above us calling aggressively as they chased a passing Heron. From the slopes of Everton Heights it became clear that there were a lot more than we had at first estimated, probably 30-40 nests. Everton Heights themselves are well worth a visit especially for the views across the river, out to sea and across to North Wales. When you see these 'new' green hills from the ferry it now looks as though the South Downs run along the horizon behind the Pier Head! One patch of wild, 'neglected' grasses that we did find was already enough to provide a haven for many wild flowers attracting Meadow Brown butterflies, Small Skippers, Burnet Moth, Cinnabar and damselflies.

Returning from a full day's Nature Watch I found a Barn Owl pellet not far from Bidston Station confirming that they were still in the area, presumably nesting.

3 JULY: First Gatekeeper butterflies. First Cinnabar caterpillars on ragwort.

4 JULY: A Leaf-Cutter Bee at work. Two more Red Admirals after first reports on 26 June.

6 JULY: PIER HEAD TO PARADISE (STREET) NATURE TRAIL: Two Common Sandpipers flew past the Pier Head landing stage along the Albert Dock 'beach'. More Blackheaded Gulls returning. Grey Wagtail back at Canning Dock. Arrived from Kings Dock area where presumably nested.

7 JULY: Buddleia starting to come into flower. A green Hawthorn Shield Bug – on hawthorn!

It was this big!

Bob Dylan, Lionel Ritchie, Ray Charles were all invited to come on this Sunday Nature Watch but they must have been otherwise engaged! We met outside BBC Radio Merseyside in Paradise Street and went round the corner to Quiggins in College Lane where Harry let us in to see where the Blackbirds had nested – in a cupboard and on a girder (see 17 April). Then across Chavasse Park where we identified the 'mystery' flowers in the Moathouse garden as Yellow Balsam – a rather rare flower of the NW – so another local speciality.

On to the 'coral reef' in Salthouse Dock where an eel was spotted in the water – 'this big' according to some! Numbers of small jellyfish increasing. I didn't expect to see any Blackbirds at the 'de Wadden' schooner so I showed the group the photos I had taken of the nests below decks. But then a male Blackbird did turn up- right on cue! It popped in through the porthole obviously feeding young from a second brood. The weather was not too kind and most of the group decided to call it a day at this point but three intrepid explorers did continue – to the Baltic Fleet. On the small 'oasis' next to the Baltic Fleet we found Meadow Brown, Small Skipper, Large White and Cinnabar caterpillars. I insisted that eight Blackheaded Gulls waiting by a puddle outside the Big Top at Kings Dock were queuing up for the evening concert. We kept on walking 'just round the next corner' until we had reached the Garden Festival site and strayed into the overgrown Japanese Garden where we found Figwort, Monkey Flower, Purple Loosestrife, Fringed Waterlilies, as well as several unidentifiable exotic 'left-overs'. Also the last Bee Orchid to be seen in flower. By now the light was fading and the bus which took us back to the city centre passed the Kings Dock where people were already assembling for the evening concert.

GATEACRE PARK DRIVE: I wrote before to say there were no sparrows here when we first moved house in August last year. I am quite delighted that yesterday a single House Sparrow came to dine at my bird table. He must have liked what he found because he came again today. I hope he brings his family and friends!

Norma Richardson

10 JULY: HAMILTON SQUARE PEREGRINES WORKING FOR CHARITY

I am writing to thank you for helping our Appeal by issuing a pamphlet about the Peregrines at Hamilton Square Station to the public who came to see them. Your kindness and support to the Hospice is very much appreciated.

Janet Coker, Claire House, Clatterbridge Hospital

On 16 July I produced a new edition of the Peregrine brochure telling the story we had been able to put together since 10 March when I had first seen the Peregrines back at the station tower. Our very first Sunday Nature Watch on 25 March was to see the Peregrines, before eggs had been laid. Our Sunday Nature Watch on 20 May coincided almost exactly with the hatching of the young and on 10 June we watched one of the young birds scratching out the last down from its plumage.

11 JULY: SWALLOWS NESTING IN MAGHULL TOWN SQUARE: There is a Swallow's nest on top of the notice hanging above the Bon Marche shop. The notice sticks out from the name above the shop at right angles. Rodney Fletcher

A GARDEN IN LIVERPOOL 14: A fatality occurred on the grass: lots of brown and grey feathers when I came home from work – not the first time this has happened. Other 'wildlife' includes a wasp's nest in the chimney – wasps keep appearing in the living room which I'm not very happy about! Margaret Parry

Margaret was still suffering from the wasps into October.

11 JULY: THE SEABIRDS OF THE GREAT ORME, Llandudno: The nearest (real) seabird colony to Liverpool – about 40 miles away as the 'sea crow' flies. In fact many of the Cormorants on the Mersey were no doubt born on the Great Orme though there is obviously an influx from outside the region too. It is virtually impossible even to estimate the numbers of birds nesting on the cliffs by the lighthouse. The following figures are the approximate numbers from last year (including the Little Orme): Guillemot 2000; Razorbill 250; Kittiwake 1700 nests; Cormorant 230; Fulmar 18. A big young Herring Gull was sitting on the step of one of the seafront hotels – a taste of things to come in Liverpool if the number of roof nesting gulls continues to increase. And a last black and red Cinnabar Moth, more or less finished on the pavement.

13 JULY: INJURED FOX ON BIDSTON MOSS: It was my turn to say thank you – to the RSPCA for their speedy assistance. I had found a young fox presumably hit by a car on the nearby road. Joanna Williams at Cross Lane RSPCA (new buildings recently opened by 'Dr Dolittle' Philip Scofield) called out the 'ubiquitous' Derek Hampson, collection officer, who took the fox away. He later told me that it had a broken back and had to be put down. Joanna told me that she had recently confronted some young boys with spades who openly admitted that they were looking for foxes. Apparently there is still no law against this sort of cruelty which surely must be bad for the children involved as well as for the foxes.

15 JULY: NATURE WATCH NEWS

Since the news that one of the young Peregrines at Hamilton Square had been killed by a bus and another taken to Thurstaston after falling into the ventilation shaft there have been several confirmations that the remaining young have continued to use the station tower and seem to be able to fend for themselves now. On 10 July the Wirral Globe reported that four pairs of Barn Owls are nesting in Wirral. One pair is only two miles or so from the Pier Head, which makes central Merseyside's list of birds even more impressive.

The pinks and purples of Rosebay and Great Hairy Willowherb, Knapweed and thistles dominate now with the white of Bramble and Privet, Bindweed and Wild Carrot. Also in flower: Evening Primrose, Himalayan Balsam, Common Toadflax,

St John's Wort, Purple Loosestrife, Scabious; both yellow and white Bedstraw and Stonecrop have been reported. Farewell to the Bee Orchids for another year: a last faded flower on 10 July with Marsh Orchids now also finishing.

There are a lot of orange Soldier Beetles, often seen on Yarrow, Vapourer Moth caterpillars on roses and bramble. Leaf-cutter Bees have been seen at work in several places and parasitic wasps attacking a Nursery Web Spider's 'nest'.

As forecast in the last Nature Watch News male Gatekeeper butterflies were reported from many places from 3 July quickly becoming numerous with a first female on 12 July. A first Comma of the new generation was reported on 9 July and regularly since then. Small Skippers were especially numerous at the beginning of July, Large Skippers have just about died off now, as have Cinnabar Moths, but there are plenty of their caterpillars on Ragwort. The first generation of Common Blues has finished but a new generation should be appearing at the end of July. In the meantime Holly Blues have been spotted again – on 15 July, last reported on 24 May. Meadow Browns and Speckled Woods should be flying through to September now and a new generation of Small Tortoiseshells has been appearing since around 10 July in increasing numbers. Red Admirals have been reported almost daily since 26 June and a new generation of Peacocks should be appearing soon just in time to take advantage of the Buddleia now coming into flower.

Most birds have stopped singing now, as noticed and confirmed by our Travel Watch expert Ron Davies. Song Thrushes will continue to sing till the end of the month: otherwise the loud song of the tiny Wren will be the only conspicuous bird song.

And autumn migration has already started! A Common Sandpiper landed for a second on the landing stage at the Pier Head on 6 July, several others reported since. Blackbirds, Mistle Thrushes, Starlings and Whitethroat on berberis berries: more signs of 'autumn'!

**SUNDAY 15 JULY:
WIRRAL SHOW AT
NEW BRIGHTON**

BBC Radio Merseyside had its own marquee at the Wirral Show and I went along on the Saturday with copies of our Nature Watch newsletters, some of my pictures and copies of my Nature Watch Diary 2000. Many BBC Radio Merseyside personalities called in during the two days – Andy Ball, Tony Snell, David Roberts, Frankie Connor, Clive Garner and, of course, the A-Team. In true Nature Watch fashion I had arrived at the showground the long way round to investigate some of the local open spaces. On the site of the old New Brighton baths I found five species of butterflies including Red Admiral and I was intrigued to see a pair of Ringed Plovers obviously on nesting territory and 'anxious' as though they had young. A Holly Blue – the first of a new generation –flew past by the Cliff where Linnets and Whitethroat were in evidence amongst the gorse and brambles. At the tent I had a marvellous opportunity to meet so many people and to chat about this and that. I received a lot of very useful information especially about the Great Crested Grebes seen regularly on the dock by the Four Bridges.

On the Sunday we met at New Brighton Station to go the long way round again - this time via the Gorse next to the Water Tower on top of the hill and down to Vale Park to get close-up views of waders on the shore which were now starting to return. Oystercatcher, Redshank, Curlew, Turnstone, Ringed Plover are the regular visitors here. On the site of the old Tower Grounds we found seven species of butterflies in the glade around the big old beech tree – including two more Holly Blues and two Commas. The Ringed Plovers were at the old New Brighton baths again and when I went back the following day I was at last able to pick out a highly camouflaged chick which had obviously been there all the time but invisible in amongst the pebbles and the gravel. Ringed Plovers nest at Seaforth Nature Reserve just across the river from New Brighton (ten pairs) but this pair nesting in urban surroundings qualified them as another Merseyside urban speciality.

Including various stops en route it took us close on seven hours to reach the BBC Radio Merseyside tent at the Wirral Show! In fact it was just closing down as we arrived. The day was rounded off with a harrier – of the noisy, jump-jet variety! The Red Arrows had already been and gone.

YOU'LL NEVER WALK ALONE: NATURE WATCH DIARY 2000

The Stargazer, Bidston Moss

Having spent much of my life chasing various birds and other kinds of wildlife around different parts of Europe I was keen to do 'something special' for the 2000 Millennium. What better than to do a new survey of the place where it had all begun -here on Merseyside - on Bidston Moss. I still had my first nature notes – from 1958 when I was a pupil at Poulton Primary School, Wallasey and I quickly saw the possibility of giving copies of the finished diary to pupils at the school in the hope that it would encourage them to take interest in their local area, just as I had been encouraged by teachers, family and friends. In the introduction I wrote: This is the story of the last fifty years. Who is going to tell the story of the next fifty years?

Gerry Marsden who I knew from earlier projects (NSPCC, Hillsborough) kindly provided a special message. Gerry was the obvious choice because every time I walked over Bidston Moss in spring listening to Skylarks I could hear the words of You'll Never Walk Alone! This is what Gerry wrote:

AND THE SWEET SILVER SONG OF A LARK…

I've got a feeling you've heard those words before! But when was the last time you heard the song of a Skylark over your head – if ever. But don't worry if you haven't: it's not your fault. There aren't so many of them about these days because a lot of the places they went to have been built on. So to see and heard Skylarks singing on Bidston Moss again is a real treat, especially when you think the lovely green hill where they sing had been a rubbish tip for about sixty years.

I hope that Robert's story of what happened on Bidston Moss in Millennium Year 2000 will make you appreciate and enjoy the world you live in and then

YOU'LL NEVER WALK ALONE !

Gerry

By 16 July copies of the Nature Watch Diary were in Poulton School ready to give to this year's school leavers when they broke up on the last day of term.

20 JULY: BRITISH OPEN AT LYTHAM ST ANNES: This major sporting event had once again come to the region bringing names like Tiger Woods with it. I had thought of doing a special Nature Watch around the golf course before or after the event but in the end I found television coverage offered a good general picture of what was going on besides the golf. A Great Tit could be heard at the 7th; a Wren singing at the 8th; Swallows flying low over the 13th green; Song Thrush song and various gulls as to be expected – mainly Blackheaded, but also Herring and Lesser Blackbacks. While everybody else was no doubt focused on the drama of Tiger Woods playing out of a bunker on the 18th for a bogey which was the beginning of the end for his hopes I was fascinated to see three or four Meadow Brown butterflies flitting over the grasses just behind him! Two eagles during the competition. Talking of eagles…

EAGLE OWL ON THE LOOSE IN BEBINGTON: Listeners had first drawn my attention to the Eagle Owl on 26 June when the Rowlands family wrote to say there was a big owl about two feet tall with big ears 'like a Long Eared Owl but much bigger' in Langdale Road. Then another letter from them dated 3 July:

"My daughters wrote to you last week about an owl; it was an Eagle Owl. We have it on video. Most of our neighbours have videoed and photographed it. We have been in touch with the rangers, police, zoos, but no luck with its owner. The RSPCA is trying to trace them. We last saw it on Sunday night (1 July) but nothing since".

Then on 16 July BBC Radio Merseyside's A-Team told me that Jan Davies had telephoned to say a big owl had been in the oak tree in her garden in the Kings Lane area of Bebington since Friday (13 July). On 24 July Jan telephoned me to say it was in the oak tree again and as we were talking she said: *'Hold on, I think it's just flown off: a big shadow went across the window....Yes, it's gone.'* That was the last report I received.

Malcolm Ingham, wildlife officer at Thurstaston, told me that it is not against the law to keep Eagle Owls and there is 'no paper work involved'. The owner was known and really it was his responsibility to catch it again if he wanted it back. But this can be very difficult because they usually enjoy their freedom and can survive quite successfully in the wild.

ANGLICAN CATHEDRAL: Two young Kestrels are now being put through their paces by their parents as they try their first flights from the nest on the west face of the cathedral.   Maurice Bray

PIER HEAD TO PARADISE (STREET) NATURE TRAIL: A Whimbrel – like a small Curlew – flew past the Pier Head and Albert Dock in typical, calm, sunny 'Whimbrel weather'. Several were seen at Seaforth Nature Reserve around the same time. Buddleia coming into flower 'everywhere' in the city centre, growing out of walls, on rooftops, in car parks.

21 JULY: PEREGRINE UPDATE: Malcolm Ingham at Thurstaston told me he still had the Peregrine which had fallen into the ventilation shaft at Woodside a month earlier. It was extremely weak still and in a very sorry state.

**SUNDAY 22 JULY:
LAST NIGHT OF THE
POPS**

We met on the steps of St George's Hall to go the long way round (again!) to Kings Dock where there was to be an evening of 'Land of Hope and Glory' with Carl Davies and the Liverpool Phil to wind up the series of Summer Pops concerts which had attracted so many big names - including a certain Tom Jones who turned up on the Monday for a final blast!

We set off up Mount Pleasant to look for the now 'famous' city centre sparrows in Cathedral Walk just below the Metropolitan Cathedral. (This was possibly the first 'scientific expedition' ever to go in search of House Sparrows!). Then we continued along Hope Street to see the young Kestrels at the Anglican Cathedral. The highlight of the day was probably the Buddleia now in flower everywhere. We decided that the 'prize winning' specimen was the one in the car park outside the 'Pulse' nightclub by Lime Street Station, but we found it in many other interesting places including the roof of the closed-down Irish Centre and one opposite Paul McCartney's LIPA school – the old Liverpool Institute where he had been himself the Friday before to present graduation certificates to students.

The buddleia easily gets a good, firm footing in the tiniest of cracks whereas some of the group said they couldn't get it to grow in the richer soil of their gardens! We went down from the cathedral, past the Chinese Gate and down Duke Street to Chavasse Park where Meadow Brown butterflies were spotted for the first time. A couple of resident Common Blues had also been seen in the wild grasses next to the car park on several occasions.

23 JULY: SEFTON PARK: The wing remains of a Great Spotted Woodpecker found in the remains of Sparrowhawk kill. A young vixen was found dead (run over) by the Alicia Hotel. The resident Sparrowhawks which have nested by Sefton Cricket Club for the past three years are not nesting there this year but are still around. Tawny Owls have territory by the cricket club, the Solna Hotel and near the café. Nuthatches chased out Blue Tits to take over their nesting hole.

Alan McGlynn

65

*The proof: the tide does
come in – sometimes – at
Southport!*

Now that the school holidays had begun BBC Radio Merseyside was offering tips and ideas for things which the whole family could do together. NATURE WATCH was one obvious possibility – just go out and explore – even in your own back garden – and you are certain to find something of interest. I met up with BBC Radio Merseyside reporter James Cameron and several listeners who came along on the bridge over the Marine Lake and although there were lots of people there that day there were probably just as many birds – ducks, geese, swans, gulls, Moorhen, Coot. We walked along the manicured lakeside where there was little of interest in the way of wildlife but then we came across a patch of wild grasses just by the pier which was being renovated. Here there were six species of butterflies including the first Common Blues of a new generation, also Burnet Moths, graphically illustrating just how important even a small patch of wild grassland can be.

For me the highlight of the day was probably the fact that the tide was in! This was the first time I can remember seeing the beach at Southport covered by the 30 ft tide.

NORTHERN LINE – MOORFIELDS TO SOUTHPORT: On the way up to Southport I made the following notes from the train:

Moorfields-Sandhills: buddleia, buddleia, buddleia; Rosebay, Rowan berries.

Bank Hall: Mulleins, Honeysuckle – Wren song.

Bank Hall-Seaforth and Litherland: St John's Wort, Japanese Knotweed, Melilot.

Waterloo-Hall Road: Bindweed, Russian Vine, lots of Golden Rod, Meadowsweet.

Hightown: "Where the River Alt meets the sea" – a big display board with a Reed Bunting in the foreground as a characteristic bird of the area. Poppies, Honeysuckle, Evening Primrose.

Formby-Freshfield: bigger trees, beech and chestnut. Another Sefton Coast display board. Why not at all stations – and other places around Liverpool and Merseyside!

Ainsdale: pine trees, field full of Ragwort, Evening Primrose, Knapweed.

Hillside: a lot of pink 'Lavetera' in gardens.

Southport: Buddleia again, Japanese Knotweed, St John's Wort, Russian Vine – Blackheaded Gulls.

27 JULY: FOREST FEVER FORTNIGHT IN FAZAKERLEY:

I almost went dizzy when I saw the impressive list of events and walks which had been organised for Forest Fever Fortnight and decided a 'Walk on the Wildside' in Fazakerley's Bluebell Woods would be the most useful addition to the Nature Watch map. We met up with rangers Andy and Paul at the hospital gates and made our way down to the woods hoping to catch a glimpse of the Red Squirrels which were the speciality here – still hanging on in this isolated outpost. However, Grey Squirrels had recently arrived and although both species seemed to be living in peaceful coexistence time would no doubt tell. There was a lot of Himalayan Balsam growing in the damp woods, Speckled Wood butterflies and a burst of Blackcap song. No sign of the woodpeckers and Nuthatches which also live here. Foxes have been seen raiding the bins at the back of the hospital. And lots of interesting stories and information about other places as well as Fazakerley.

PIER HEAD TO PARADISE (STREET) NATURE TRAIL: That morning I found Small Skipper, Meadow Brown, Small White and Small Tortoiseshell on the grasses and flowers by the law courts. About 300 Starlings were on the small patch of 'wasteland' by the Baltic Fleet – almost knocking me over when they flew up! I couldn't believe that so many birds could be packed into such a small place. Ants were probably the attraction. A Common Blue of the second generation was flying as well as a Latticed Heath Moth and two Meadow Browns. Cinnabar caterpillars on ragwort. Three Grey Wagtails flying over were clearly a family group.

PRINCES DOCK: After the morning broadcast I went up to explore the dockland to the north of Princes Dock. Gatekeepers and Meadow Browns were flying, one Common Blue. Not much in the way of birds but in the distance I could hear an anxious Ringed Plover and with binoculars I was able to make out an adult, obviously on nesting territory with a chick somewhere close by as we had found at New Brighton. This was one much closer to the Pier Head – not much more than half a mile away!

ST MICHAEL'S HAMLET: I've just seen three Mistle Thrushes – the first time I've seen them here near Priory Woods. Ivor Scholes

A sign, perhaps, that Mistle Thrushes are continuing to prosper and expand.

PARKGATE MARSHES: Approximately midday. While walking the children on this extremely hot day we witnessed a 'blizzard' of birds over the marsh. It was a wonderful and fascinating sight. It was like a moving cloud, a sort of huge visual tornado of birds – the shape kept altering and twisting, one direction then another, It was a thrilling experience. Can anyone tell me what they were? Val Curtis

Does it really matter what they were, so long as they made such a deep impression!? Probably Dunlin at this time of the year and a sign that wader migration was already well under way.

SUNDAY 29 JULY: PORT SUNLIGHT – NEW FERRY BUTTERFLY PARK

This Nature Watch opened our eyes to the fine variety of trees in the Dell hitherto unnoticed even by some local residents, including such exotic species as false Acacia and Honey Locust Tree! House Martins were obviously nesting somewhere close by and a group of screaming Swifts was one of the last times they were seen before their departure at the beginning of August. The gardens of Port Sunlight were bright with colour in anticipation of this year's Britain in Bloom competition which they had won twice in recent years. But they offered very little in the way of wildlife whereas just across the road by Bebington Station the butterfly park was 'buzzing' with damselflies and dragonflies as well as bees and butterflies, ten species in all including Holly Blue and Small Copper. Amongst the great variety of wild flowers Viper's Bugloss caught my eye – introduced but still the only place I've seen it on Merseyside. We had such a good day - thanks to Mel Roberts and crew - we decided there was no need to dash off to catch up with the Vintage Car Rally and rangers' 'road show' in Arrowe Park.

A WALK FROM TOWN GREEN TO LYDIATE: The hedgerows were full of wild flowers – brambles, tufted vetch, bindweed, willowherbs, hedge parsley and shiny leaves of bryony. Ragwort was everywhere, in hedgerows and fields where scented mayweed, charlock, hedge mustard and sorrel were growing between fields of carrots and beans. There were various types of thistles along the paths as well as burdock, fat hen, poppies and speedwell, not to mention nettles which had taken over some of the paths when they had been closed due to foot and mouth disease.   Margaret Parry

SEFTON PARK: On a visit to Fazakerley Woods I was handed your newsletter. Long time since I've had so much local nature news! Yellow Balsam is also growing in Ibbotson's Lane and Moschatel (Town Hall Clock) at the corner of Lark Lane and Livingston Avenue. At St Michael's Hamlet - next to Pleasure Island – Buttonweed is growing in a shallow pool on the left hand side of the coach park. Originally from South Africa it is common around Leasowe Lighthouse, but rare here – and in the rest of Britain.   Walter Roughsedge

31 JULY NATURE WATCH NEWS

Since finishing the last Nature Watch News on a note of autumn (birds on berries, first migrating Common Sandpipers) there has been a 'second spring' as far as the butterflies are concerned. As predicted, the first 'new' Common Blues were seen on 25 July, the first Peacocks a day later. Holly Blues have also been reported regularly since 15 July and a Small Copper was seen on 29 July, the first since 20 June. Small Tortoiseshells, Meadow Browns, Gatekeepers, Small Skippers, Speckled Woods and Whites have all been profiting from the fine warm weather of the last ten days. Red Admirals will probably not be seen now until a new generation appears towards the end of August. One report only of a migrant Painted Lady.

The big news from the region was the first successful breeding of Little Egrets - at Frodsham, just 13 miles from the Pier Head. Only a few years ago the nearest would have been about 700 miles away in the South of France! Also Avocets nesting for the first time at Leighton Moss and Ospreys in the Lake District. These – and Red Kite as close as Denbigh – suggested that the birds were deliberately closing in on Merseyside in response to our dream of turning Merseyside into the biggest – and the best – the only Metropolitan Wildlife Park in the country!

Ringed Plovers have nested just north of Prince's Dock, as well as those found at New Brighton. On 16 July I produced a new edition of my Peregrines at Hamilton Square brochure telling this year's story. Since then I've seen a single Peregrine on and around the ventilation tower by the river on 18 and 29 July.

Barn Owls have been feeding young for over three weeks now and an Eagle Owl has been on the loose in Bebington since at least 26 June. I'm told by the 'authorities' that it is perfectly legal and that there is little they can do about it as it is obviously enjoying its freedom. Great Crested Grebes can be seen by the Four Bridges in Birkenhead Docks, a tip-off I was given at the Wirral Show. Grey Wagtails which I had been trying to pin down in Albert Dock before they disappeared, have turned up again, almost certainly having nested somewhere around the Queen's Dock – Baltic Fleet, so we can claim several pairs of city centre Grey Wagtails on both sides of the river. On 20 July a Whimbrel flew past Albert Dock and the Pier Head. On 25 July a Kingfisher was at the pools by Bidston Station so expect a blue flash on canals, even park lakes now. Up to 11 Herons on the roof of 'Comet' easily seen by commuters approaching Birkenhead North Station. Also on 25 July I was able to get up to the RSPB reserve at Marshside – close enough to Southport to be urban nature watching?! The highlights were four Ruff and a Common Sandpiper as well as the many Greylag Geese and Canadas which are now flying again after a month of flightless moult. On 27 July Linda (McDermott) almost fell off her seat when I turned up in the studio wearing my home-made Red Indian headdress, courtesy of local Canada Geese! A lot of Sea Holly from Southport to Marshside. Red Squirrels and a fine display of Himalayan Balsam in Fazakerley's Bluebell Woods. Watch out for evening flocks of screaming Swifts, preparing to leave in the next few days. And for Blackheaded Gulls going up and 'hawking' silently for flying ants on warm, sultry days – if we get them, that is!

PIER HEAD TO PARADISE (STREET) NATURE TRAIL
ALBERT DOCK   KINGS DOCK   CHAVASSE PARK

My 'promise' of 50 species of birds within a mile of the Liver Birds at the Pier Head had already been fulfilled when the Swifts arrived at the beginning of May. If a birdwatcher had been shown the list, which included Peregrine, Buzzard, Raven, Grey Wagtail, Lapwing, Ringed Plover and Skylark, he would probably have thought we were talking about some idyllic corner of North Wales, the Pennines or the Lake District. But this was all around the Ferry Cross The Mersey landing stages at the Pier Head, Seacombe and Woodside, the very heart of built-up Merseyside! Then there were the local 'beaches' including the Albert Dock-Kings Dock 'beach' with waders such as Oystercatcher, Redshank, Dunlin, Turnstone, Curlew, Common Sandpiper and even a Whimbrel on 20 July. Ringed Plovers were obviously nesting at the Clarence Dock site where Mute Swans had also nested as well as Lapwings, Linnets and Skylarks, possibly Shelduck. Most of the common garden birds that could be expected were nesting in or around Chavasse Park, the Bluecoat, the Baltic Fleet.

Both Herring Gulls and Lesser Blackbacks were nesting on rooftops at the Pier Head, Derby Square etc. The most successful bird – after Starlings, pigeons and gulls – was probably the Mistle Thrush rather than Blackbird – at least four pairs around Chavasse Park alone with many more not far away. Greenfinches and Goldfinches were always conspicuous and we had the specialities of Blackbirds nesting below decks in the 'de Wadden' schooner and inside Quiggins. Starlings nesting in the lights on the masts of the Edmund Gardner pilot boat. Pied and Grey Wagtails. But no House Sparrows, an absence which reflected the situation in most other city centres.

Not only birds, of course. A fascinating variety of wild flowers had been found – most notably the Yellow Balsam growing in the Moathouse garden – a rare flower of the NW. Teasel, Melilot, Wild Pansy, Purple Toadflax, Hemp Agrimony and lots of buddleia were other 'specialities' of note. Most sensational of all were the thirty or so Marsh Orchids found growing just down the road from BBC Radio Merseyside in Paradise Street on the corner of Canning Place, visible from the reception window! Then the Bee Orchids in the car park opposite the Daily Post and Echo and just off Leeds Street. Don't forget the magnificent plane trees at the Bluecoat and the Bluecoat courtyard.

Common Blue butterflies were found in both Chavasse Park and at the Baltic Fleet. Large Whites, Meadow Browns, Small Skipper, Small Tortoiseshell, Cinnabar Moth and Latticed Heath Moth were also found. A migrant Red Admiral flew along the Pier Head on 6 July.

The docks provided us with our very own 'aquarium'- a coral reef with sea anemones and crabs on the side of the landing stage in Salthouse Dock. Jellyfish and eels and no doubt much more which remained undetected. A Grey Seal was seen from the ferry just off the Pier Head on at least one occasion.

What had started as a bit of a joke – to proclaim Merseyside the first Metropolitan Wildlife Park in the country – was starting to become a serious proposition!

SUNDAY 5 AUGUST : VIKINGS v SAXONS IN ARROWE PARK

As the bloody fight began we scanned the sky for vultures

The Merseyside International Street Festival was reaching its finale at Albert Dock but we just had to get involved in the historic brawl that was taking place across the river!

Families of Swallows were circling and swooping, the young enjoying their new-found skill in flying. The dainty ballerina-like Pied Wagtail danced along the path while a chubby young Robin gazed about at this wonderful world. We looked at flowers with such intriguing names as Fat Hen and Good King Henry. They were both once eaten as a form of spinach, so the Vikings we had come to see could have been eating Good King Henry in Arrowe Park a long time ago!

Coffee time beckoned, an excuse just to sit and enjoy the sun, cloud gazing. Amazing the pictures we could find – feathers, Viking spears, even the cross of St Andrew. Butterflies were the next interest. A Comma spread its multi-patterned wings while Gatekeepers, male and female, fluttered by.

The Kingfisher eluded us but we heard a Green Woodpecker calling just above our heads and watched huge fish in the lake (carp?).

A memorable day, I'm glad the Vikings brought me to Arrowe Park that Sunday morning.
Dorothy Wardley

WARNING: BIRDS CROSSING! Just a few notes from my cycle ride early Friday morning. Just before Arrowe Brook Farm I sighted a humorous but heartfelt notice: **Warning! Give these birds a chance. Ducks and Moorhens cross here! SLOW DOWN.** It gave me such a ripple of pleasure and amusement to see it. What a brilliant and caring thing to do!
Val Curtis

8 AUGUST: YELLOWHAMMER – AT LAST! On a walk from Storeton to Landican I was delighted – and relieved - to hear a Yellowhammer singing in the fields between Landican and Thingwall. Several listeners had provided 'anecdotal' accounts of Yellowhammers along the Wirral Way, around Tarbock and in Formby, but no precise locations. Later I realised that this was probably because of foot and mouth restrictions: people hadn't been going out into the agricultural areas where Yellowhammers are normally found. This one was just on 4½ miles from the Pier Head.

SUNDAY 12 AUGUST: SEAFORTH NATURE RESERVE

The heavy rain was no problem: we had the luxury of three hides to choose from with a scene before us as fascinating as any African safari you will see on TV. A Heron fishing in one corner; 60 or more Cormorants resting on the edge of the pool. Ten species of waders including Black Tailed Godwit, Lapwing and Golden Plover. Common Sandpiper, Dunlin and Ringed Plover came feeding right in front of the hide and a pair of Kittiwakes landed and preened on a post almost within arm's reach! House Martins and Swifts were skimming low over the water; a fox came hunting out in the open scattering rabbits. Pochard and Tufted Ducks diving, Mute Swans, a flock of Canada Geese. It was like being in a different world and yet we were only four miles from the Pier Head! No Wall Brown butterflies – a speciality here – but we did find six Common Blues sheltering close together from the rain. And all this with the constant noise of 172 pairs of nesting Common Terns all around us. A dream!

THE WHITE WINGED CROWS OF MERSEYSIDE:

SEFTON PARK: There has been a pair of Carrion Crows nesting in Sefton Park for the past few years. One of the adults has white wing tips and at least one of their young has the same white markings each year. I have just watched one adult with three young, two with the white wing tips and the third 'pied', looking more like a Magpie than a Crow!
Alan McGlynn

We saw a young 'white winged' Crow in Arrowe Park on our Sunday Nature Watch on 5 August and also near the Garden Festival site on 8 July. I had already been watching two families of Crows in the Bidston Moss area with the same wing pattern and I was told that this went back at least three generations. Others have been seen in Moreton and New Brighton. On our Sunday Nature Watch on 24 June John, who lives on the edge of Bidston Hill, told us that such genetic defects become 'diluted' with each generation and eventually disappear. But the defect seems to be so 'dominant' on Merseyside we have reserved the subspecies name Corvus corone merseyensis – just in case!

MAGPIES BUILDING BARBED WIRE FORTRESS: This year a pair of Magpies built a nest high up inside the entrance to Asda, Bromborough. I first noticed it when I started finding pieces of barbed wire and 'other mess' on the floor below.
Mike Dinsmore

Pigeons have been known to make nests out of ordinary wire in the past – just behind BBC Radio Merseyside – but barbed wire is obviously the ideal substitute for the thorny twigs which Magpies normally use. What next!

PIER HEAD TO PARADISE (STREET) NATURE TRAIL: I went out looking for nettles! There is so much buddleia in the city centre which normally attracts butterflies such as Small Tortoiseshell, Peacock and Red Admiral, all of which lay their eggs exclusively on nettles. But of all the 'weeds' I found in the city centre nettles seem to be 'exceedingly rare'! If we want the butterflies to exploit the buddleia we need more nettles, so can we have some nettle plantations strategically located round car parks etc. in the city centre please!

15 AUGUST : NATURE WATCH NEWS

The ten-day heat wave came to an abrupt end on 2 August: torrential rain on 6-7 August, then 13-15 August 'heavy' and humid with a lot of flying ants going up though not many Blackheaded Gulls seen chasing them this year. The speciality of Common Gulls, now returning, along the North Wirral coast is not 'anting' but cockling: they have learnt to crack open cockles by dropping them from some height onto the concrete embankment – so mind your heads!

The Swifts have gone – always a major milestone in the Nature Watch calendar. Groups of Swifts were still screaming round their nesting sites at the beginning of August but by the end of the first week they had disappeared 'overnight'. There was a strong passage of migrating Swifts 11-14 August but now there will only be the occasional stragglers into September. So, see you next May!

Many House Martins stay on into October but their main passage and departure is also underway now. They will roost in quite large numbers on towers, including blocks of flats, warming themselves in the early morning sun, clinging to the wall. Last year on 24 August I counted about 200 on the ventilation tower at Seacombe Ferry, a favourite spot, it seems. Willow Warblers have been turning up in gardens on migration, so listen out for an 'oo-ee' call in the trees and bushes. Most of them gone by the end of August.

Gardens may seem quiet now but I have found Blackcaps and Whitethroats sneaking in unannounced and Blackbirds hidden silently in bushes and trees after berries or pecking at apples. A flock of over 200 Greenfinches out in harvested fields tells you where your Greenfinches have gone! Mistle Thrushes are starting to concentrate on Rowan berries now.

The last report of Song Thrush song was on 3 August and even the usually noisy Wren has been quiet the last week or so. But Robins are starting to sing their autumn song as they stake out winter territories.

A Painted Lady butterfly was on the buddleia outside Wallasey Village Library on 14 August. There have only been a couple of reports this year compared with the big influx last year but watch out for more now into September. The next day, instead of a Painted Lady, there was a Red Admiral by the library, the first of the new generation, earlier than last year. As well as buddleia, which will be finishing soon, they like Ice Plants and Michaelmas Daisies, just starting. The Painted Ladies prefer thistles if they can get them. In fact a total of 17 species of butterflies reported this month, including Wall Brown at Seaforth and Hightown. I saw 12 species myself in about one hour on 15 August, including a late Small Skipper and a Small Heath, a surprise because I hadn't been expecting to see any more this year. Holly Blue still flying. Gatekeepers will be finished by the end of the month.

SUNDAY 19 AUGUST
PENNY LANE

We met 'behind the shelter in the middle of the roundabout' but there were only a few glimpses of 'blue suburban skies'. In fact the highlight of the day was a massive thunderstorm, but with impeccable timing, due no doubt to the skill of our leader, we had reached the cafe in Sefton Park just in time to dive inside to avoid the heaviest downpour of the summer.

When you cross the railway bridge in Penny Lane you come into a different world: suburban skies give way to a canopy of tall mature trees continuing along Ibbotson's Lane and into the Dell. There were plenty of rabbits nibbling away at the grass of Liverpool College's playing field and there were stands of Wood Avens or Herb Bennet. Apparently the roots were used to flavour ale or as an insect repellent or maybe both together! There was also some Enchanter's Nightshade which was named Aelfthone by the Anglo-Saxons and was used as a protection against elves. (You don't see many elves these days so I suppose it must work!).

The vegetation was lush as we reached the Dell (Turkey Oak and a Chestnut tree – where Joe's wife used to collect conkers). Plenty of White and Speckled Wood butterflies but the highlight in the park was the woodpecker's nest hole and, about two feet away in the same tree, a Nuthatch's nest hole. No sign of the woodpecker but we did see the Nuthatch and later the nest of the Tree Creeper in a crevice in an old birch tree which Bob had found on Easter Sunday.

On the lake there was a large, rather untidy Coot's nest and plenty of male Mallards keeping a low profile for a change while they moulted. Several dragonflies skimmed over the surface and we watched a young fisherman examine his catch before he returned it to the lake.

After the storm we emerged from the café refreshed to follow the stream up to the Grotto passing Water Plantain with tall stems but tiny flowers, Purple Loosestrife and Marestail.

Margaret Parry – with a little help from her friends!

INTERNATIONAL BEATLES FESTIVAL

SUNDAY 26 AUGUST: STRAWBERRY FIELD

Let me take you down….

There was a noticeable influx – of visitors from abroad! En route we met people from Finland, France, US and most of all Japan. A Wren was singing loud at Strawberry Field gates and there were big ripe blackberries and Foxglove (gone to seed) near John Lennon's house in Menlove Avenue. Ice Plants, Michaelmas Daisies, Ivy-Leaved Toadflax – and Himalayan Balsam down a back alley in Woolton Village. At St Peter's church hall we bumped into Graham Paisley, verger at St Peter's, with a busload of Japanese visitors, some in kimonos, so we were all able to view the famous stage where 'John met Paul'. Graham then kindly took us to Eleanor Rigby's grave – where a Holly Blue butterfly was flying round the holly tree next to the church. A Grey Squirrel, lots of Yellow Balsam, some Enchanter's Nightshade again and a Speckled Wood butterfly as we crossed to Paul McCartney's house in Forthlin Road. No Blackbird Singing at this time of the year but plenty of strange languages being spoken when a Magical Mystery Tour bus turned up. By the end of the day we had the feeling we had been Here, There and Everywhere !

Dear Bob,   *29 August*

Living in an urban area often gives the impression that all we see is pigeons and of course the Liver Birds on top of the Liver Building. Your account of life in Liverpool in Nature Watch News certainly shows that this is not the case.

Strawberry Field is lucky being set in such a beautiful environment with many opportunities for the young people to enjoy the wildlife in our grounds, including a family of foxes and each year a family of ducks.

The picture you have kindly sent out to us now has pride of place in our main lounge together with all the Beatles memorabilia which we own. In its guilt-edged frame it certainly looks right in its new home.

God bless , Kathleen Renton,

Officer in Charge, Strawberry Field

27 AUGUST: SEACOMBE SUB-MARINE AQUARIUM: No, not the yellow one: that's over in Chavasse Park! As the ferry commentary says, the aquarium gives you a glimpse of the secret world that lurks beneath the Mersey. One noisy, splashing tank at the entrance recreates the tidal conditions in the river and has large Sea Bass apparently enjoying it. Lots of Flounder, flat fish which disguise themselves in the sand. Corkwing Wrasse, fish which go 'grazing' seaweed in rock pools. Dogfish – like miniature sharks – and a tank where you could see the baby dogfish wriggling in their egg cases, soon ready to emerge. The star of the show must be the Conger Eel about a metre long which Chris feeds on squid. Most of the time its body is hidden in the pipes provided with only the 'beady' eyes and head peering out! Well worth a visit.

HOYLAKE LIFEBOAT OPEN DAY: I was one of the thousands of people who went to Hoylake on Bank Holiday Monday for the Open Day. As the tide came in I saw a big white Gannet on the water being carried in along the channel by the tide. I presume it must have been sick or injured.   Tony Craven

ALBINO SWALLOWS – IN BOWRING PARK AND THURSTASTON: Tony also told me that he had recently seen a pure white Swallow over a pool in Bowring Park – an incredible coincidence because I had just been on the phone to Sheila Colley at the farm in Thurstaston Village who had just told me that they had had an albino Swallow this year!

TREE SPARROWS IN THURSTASTON: I had phoned Sheila for confirmation that it *was* Tree Sparrows she had reported, as they were now very scarce. "They're the ones with the brown heads, aren't they?" she said. Yes, they are. " Well, there's two of them on the bird table at this very moment." Enough said, no better confirmation necessary!

HOUSE MARTINS IN GARSTON: If you walk down Window Lane in Garston, the House Martins love nesting under the old corpy houses there and in Lincoln Street, Chesterton Street. But I notice it's only the old corpy houses where they build their lovely nests! I love just standing, watching them feeding on the wing; never seen them on the ground.   Muriel Hammond

GARSWOOD, St Helens: On the way down from Billinge Beacon heading back to Garswood there were Swallows lined up on the wires in several places - a sign of autumn on the way.   Margaret Parry

NETHERTON: The other day I cleared some weed out of our pond to make the fish more visible. The following morning a Heron was having a goldfish breakfast.

                                    Joe Ellis

Well, you certainly achieved your aim, Joe!

ORMSKIRK: My geriatric Kestrel (see 1 May) is losing her lovely feathery pantaloons. One leg is almost bald but she is about ten years old. She didn't produce any young this year, an event we looked forward to each year.   Thelma Westell

31 AUGUST : NATURE WATCH NEWS

Autumn migration is well underway now: Wheatears on Hilbre Island and the North Wirral coast where Swallows have also been on the move. A Spotted Flycatcher on Bidston Moss on 27 August and Dunlin were heard passing over the city on the clear night of 22 August. As mentioned in the last Nature Watch News House Martins were around the ventilation tower at Seacombe Ferry again, well over 100 birds – with another 50 around Wallasey Town Hall – on 23-24 August but none there on 31 August. An American Ring-Billed Gull has been attracting twitchers to Otterspool prom and a Great White Egret on the Dee, most often seen off Flint Castle. Albino Swallows have been reported from both Thurstaston and Bowring Park.

On 21 August Linda McDermott joined the Parkgate high tide watch when three Peregrines, a Merlin and a Hen Harrier were seen as well as various waders on migration. On the same day (team work!) I watched the high tide on Hilbre Island where a beautiful white Gannet came fishing off the north end along with about ten of the Grey Seals from the West Hoyle Bank. The tide covered Red Rocks completely, forcing Oystercatchers and other waders to seek noisy refuge on Middle Eye. Amongst the waders, two Common Sandpipers.

Another Common Sandpiper turned up at Queen's Dock, Wapping on 24 August. The day before, an escaped budgie at the Pier Head was given a hard time by local Starlings. I had just been up to the top of the Liver Building to say hello to the Liver Birds, the central symbols of our BBC Radio Merseyside Nature Watch. Unique views. A must.

Robins are singing regularly again but along with Wrens they are just about the only birds you will hear singing until Christmas when the first Blackbirds may be singing again. But listen out for Blackcaps which could be planning to stay the winter. They make a 'tick' call, similar to a Robin but harsher, more 'check'.

Two female Gatekeeper butterflies on 29 August were almost certainly the last of the year and Meadow Browns should be finished before the next Nature Watch News (15 Sept). There have now been four reports of Painted Ladies since a first on 14 August, Peacocks still flying on 28 August and more reports of Red Admirals. Common Blues are still going strong and Small Tortoiseshells were very numerous in the last week of August. They should be flying until the end of September. Last year three records in October and one on 3 November! Small Coppers should also be flying until October – if you can find these tiny gems! And watch out for more Commas now – last year until 4 October. One was already seen on 25 August. Another Small Heath on 28-29 August. Sea Bass were seen jumping in the river off Seacombe Ferry. A Buzzard over Wallasey Village on 29 August.

SUNDAY 2 SEPT: LEASOWE LIGHTHOUSE OPEN DAY

We headed for the breakwater at Leasowe Bay where large numbers of waders roost the tide, mainly Oystercatchers and Redshanks, but also Turnstone, Ringed Plover, Sanderling and other waders such as Grey Plover. The whole of the North Wirral coast has been given SSSI status (site of special scientific interest) like Seaforth Nature Reserve and the Mersey Shore from New Brighton to Seacombe and Rock Ferry to New Ferry. The Mersey and Dee estuaries themselves are 'Ramsar' sites- wetlands of international importance deserving special protection.

Suddenly hundreds of waders flew up from the breakwater and the air was filled with a cloud of piping Oystercatchers, clearly alarmed. "Peregrine!" somebody shouted and then we saw the shape of a big brown female Peregrine which had flown out unnoticed at sea level and was now twisting and turning as it singled out one of the smaller waders. This continued for a minute or so then the Peregrine gave up – too easily we thought – and carried on along the coast. But the performance was repeated about half an hour later when we were walking along the tide line looking at the egg cases of whelks and skate, razorshells and masses of feathers from moulting gulls. Again the Peregrine had no luck.

An extended coffee break meant that we were just too late to go up to the top of the lighthouse, but we were still able to enjoy the view – via CCTV on the ground floor!

It was such a good day, I went back again next day. But the Peregrine didn't show up – confirming that it had been a 'one-off' performance specially for our BBC Radio Merseyside Sunday Nature Watch - as I had claimed all along!

MUNICH: GERMANY 1 LIVERPOOL 5: The Sunday Nature Watch was the day after all England's goals in this historic World Cup qualifier had been scored by Liverpool players: Michael Owen, of course, with a nonchalant hat-trick, Steven Gerard and Emile Heskey. Now that we've got that out of the way I can point out that it was a wildlife story that made the front page headlines in the Daily Post that morning with a photo of a male Chaffinch rather than one of Michael Owen!

SHAMEFUL TRADE IN WILD BIRDS

The article claimed that Merseyside and Cheshire were being targeted by illegal bird traffickers who export finches to sell on foreign black markets, though I had heard the same story from East Anglia several months earlier, suggesting that it was a nationwide problem, rather than Merseyside and Cheshire alone. The traders use various methods to trap hundreds of birds which can fetch as much as £100 each in other parts of Europe. The Thursday before (30 August) BBC2 had shown a programme with John Humphrys looking at the illegal trade in Britain's wild birds – said to be the most profitable criminal activity after drug smuggling (?) – featuring undercover investigations carried out by the RSPCA. On 19 June Merseyside Partners Against Wildlife Crime (MPAWC) had been launched: police, RSPCA, RSPB and other organisations coming together to fight illegal fishing, egg collecting and other wildlife crime.

The 'prize winning' buddleia. Adelphi Hotel in background

'Spirit of the Jaguar' Chester Zoo

September storms on the Mersey – from New Brighton to Albert Dock

5 SEPT: NATURE WATCH MEETS HOLLYWOOD STAR STEFANIE POWERS

First Frankie goes to Hollywood – now Nature Watch – well, almost! Stefanie Powers (Hart to Hart) was at Chester Zoo to open the new tropical rainforest exhibit called the Spirit of the Jaguar – sponsored by Jaguar cars. Stefanie said it was vital that the business sector got involved in the sponsorship of such big projects but I asked her what our BBC Radio Merseyside listeners could do themselves. *"We all have to stop and think about the way we live."* Dr Alan Rabinowicz, the world's leading expert on jaguars in the wild said that Chester Zoo was a world leader in the way it linked its zoo work with conservation programmes both at home and abroad (e.g. Sand Lizards on the Sefton Coast) and that education was the key to saving our environment.

On Friday's broadcast I said that our local environment needs just as much protection as tropical rainforests abroad – for people and wildlife alike. There are lots of places of great value in the Merseyside region which need saving. I hoped that more companies and developers would follow Jaguar's example and give the local environment and wildlife priority over profit.

6 SEPTEMBER:LEACH'S PETRELS– ANOTHER MERSEYSIDE SPECIALITY

At this time of the year many seabirds are blown inshore by westerly or north-westerly gales, amongst them Leach's Petrels, only the size of a Starling, which spend most of their lives out in the Atlantic. Sometimes large numbers are seen if conditions are right as they move away from their breeding grounds on remote islands in the north of Scotland and Iceland. On 6 September a skua was also seen on the water, a Black Tern and a Kittiwake. More Leach's Petrels the following day and best of all on 13 September several were seen close in just off Seacombe Ferry landing stage with the ferry and Liver Buildings as a back drop! A lot of Common Terns were also on the river that day.

BOOTLE: I've just found a beautiful butterfly with big rings on it, especially blue – in my mop bucket in the garage. What is it and what is it doing there?

Margaret Ratcliffe

From Margaret's description it was obviously a Peacock which had decided that her mop bucket would be the best place to hibernate for the coming winter!

NETHERTON: A man on the canal asked me where all the male Mallards had gone. I was able to explain that they were still there – in disguise, having lost their colour and gone uniform brown while they moulted. Joe Ellis

7 SEPTEMBER: PIER HEAD TO PARADISE (STREET) NATURE TRAIL: A couple of Robins in Chavasse Park, new arrivals, were a sign of autumn. Grey Wagtails now being seen regularly again around Albert Dock and other parts of town. Lots of gulls on Chavasse Park at first light – some of them young birds still begging for food from parents.

SUNDAY 9 SEPT: 300 BLACK TAILED GODWITS ON NEW FERRY SHORE

It was a wonderful surprise to find so many of these majestic birds along the water's edge of the incoming tide. The Rock Ferry-New Ferry shore has only recently been declared a site of special scientific interest largely because of the godwits and other waders. We saw Oystercatcher, Redshank, Curlew, Dunlin, Sanderling, Ringed Plover, also about 12 Teal and a few Shelduck. Twenty or more Greater Blackbacked Gulls were another surprise. Charlotte (aged 6) found live crabs and amongst the interesting wild flowers were Common Fleabane, Red Bartsia and Feverfew as a garden flower in Rock Park. We also spotted a clump of Ice Plants, popular with late summer butterflies and a Red Admiral flew up to prove it! Hazel nuts, eaten presumably by the Grey Squirrel we saw.

11 SEPTEMBER 2001: The day the world was stunned and shattered by the news and pictures of what had happened in New York and Washington. It seemed the world would never be the same again. I could not help reflecting that the other creatures of this world had the advantage of being oblivious and largely unaffected by the problems of mankind. The words of Stefanie Powers came back to me from 5 September at Chester Zoo.

12 SEPTEMBER: KIRKDALE: I usually have about 20 sparrows and other birds but they have all deserted me. Where have they gone?   Cath Gordon

I promised to investigate and found about 20 sparrows in the bushes at the corner of South Park in Hawthorne Road about 400 yards from Cath's house – not necessarily Cath's sparrows but enough to put her mind at rest that they hadn't disappeared completely. They did eventually return ... as promised!

13 SEPTEMBER: RAVEN BACK AT ANGLICAN CATHEDRAL: This morning I saw one of the Ravens back on the cathedral tower where it was attracting the wrath of 11 Magpies and the local Kestrel.   Maurice Bray, clerk of works

14 SEPTEMBER: SCOTLAND ROAD: Friday's Morning Merseyside was a live broadcast from Scotland Road about the plans to create an 'urban village' community. Most obvious that morning were the many Robins, some singing (local residents?) others 'ticking' (new arrivals?). It had been a very calm, clear starry night.

15 SEPTEMBER : NATURE WATCH NEWS

No need to go hungry at this time of the year – the birds certainly aren't: blackberries, elderberries, hawthorn, rowan; plenty of insects and seeds – which explains why many listeners have been asking where their garden birds have all gone. During the summer, parties of tits have been galavanting through the trees of parks and woodland. It is not unusual to see up to 30-40 birds, usually mainly Long Tailed Tits, but Blue Tits, Great Tits, Coal Tit, Nuthatches, even Chiffchaffs and Goldcrests often join these bands of 'merry men'. Blue Tits are now starting to come back 'home' in expectation of nuts through the winter. Blackbirds have been very silent, hidden in hawthorns or elderberries which are also being guzzled by Starlings, Woodpigeons, even Crows and Blackcaps still with us. Robins reported returning to gardens since the last week of August. Even House Sparrows in some places go 'on holiday' to help with the harvest and may seem to have disappeared for a while.

Grey Wagtails are being seen or heard over all parts of Merseyside now as they disperse from nesting territories. First Meadow Pipits were passing over on 14 September – more to follow in the coming weeks. Big movement of Meadow Pipits expected at the end of the month. A migrant Wheatear was in Walton Hall Park on 14 September where breeding of Great Crested Grebes was confirmed again (3 miles from Pier Head). A bat, presumably Pipistrelle, was out flying in the sunshine at one o'clock on 11 September over the ponds in Central Park, Wallasey – one of this year's young that hadn't got the message that bats are only supposed to fly at night? Any 'oo-ee' calls from bushes or trees are now more likely to be Chiffchaff than Willow Warblers, some of them planning to stay the winter. Of the other summer migrants only Blackcap, Reed Warbler, House Martin and Swallow are still with us.

We can expect a last peak of Swallow movement any time now, most of them gone by the end of the month. So too House Martins though quite a few usually stay on into October. One was chirruping from the snug shelter of its nest in New Brighton during northerly gales on 7-8 September while Leach's Petrels – not a lot bigger than House Martins and similar coloration – were out in it, being lashed by wind and spray at the mouth of the Mersey. (Come to think of it, so was I!). There was also a Black Tern, as well as many Common Terns heading for West Africa and a skua was on the water being carried by the tide up towards the Pier Head. More gales on 13 September and fabulous views of Leach's Petrels just off Seacombe with the ferry and the Pier Head in the background. Meanwhile, back on dry land, at least 80 species of wild flowers may still be showing colour according to the books. Michaelmas Daisies becoming dominant on 'wasteland'. Speckled Woods 'everywhere' at the beginning of the month but starting to die off now, like most butterflies. Small numbers of Red Admirals being seen regularly in gardens. On 6 September a last (?) Peacock was seen disappearing into a mop bucket in Bootle to hibernate. Last Meadow Brown reported on 11 September. Male Mallards are getting back their green heads and colouring after the long summer moult.

SUNDAY 16 SEPT: GRASSENDALE AND OTTERSPOOL PROMS

The day after BBC Radio Merseyside's Roger Phillips had hosted Liverpool's contribution to the BBC's Last Night of the Proms. Next morning we met at Aigburth Station to explore our own proms at Otterspool and Grassendale! Just outside the station 18 Long Tailed Tits flew out of a tree, one by one. A summer Swallow and an autumn Meadow Pipit flew out across the Mersey and a Kestrel was resting on a lamp post. When the tide started to recede waders began to arrive on the rocky shore off Grassendale Esplanade, mainly Redshanks, Turnstone, Ringed Plover, also Dunlin, Curlew and three Shelduck. The Dolphin, Kittiwake and Kite we saw didn't count: they were the names of a ship, the pilot launch and a kite being flown at Otterspool prom! An enjoyable day.   Joe Ellis

18 SEPTEMBER: RED ROCKS, Hoylake: On 'Morning Merseyside' BBC Radio Merseyside's Simon Moffat interviewed head ranger Martyn Jamieson at Red Rocks which had just been designated a special area of conservation. Martyn said: we hear a lot about rainforests disappearing but our estuaries also need saving as vital habitats for large numbers of birds and other wildlife. (See also my comments on 5 September).

20 SEPTEMBER: BRIDGWATER CANAL, Lymm: We have cruised through several swirlings of Swallows – always near the telephone wires. One day I *will* get a photo of a Heron. When the camera is ready they always fly ahead, but sit and pose when it isn't!   Edmund and Irene Jelley

21 SEPTEMBER: PIER HEAD TO PARADISE (STREET) NATURE TRAIL: At least five Robins around Chavasse Park were a reflection of the influx of Robins noticeable everywhere. A Blackbird was noisy for the first time since summer. About 150 gulls on Chavasse Park until disturbed by first people crossing the park on the way to work. Young gulls no longer begging and squealing as they had been two weeks earlier. Three, possibly four, Grey Wagtails in the graving docks, some chasing and display, probably trying to secure winter territories.

LEEDS-LIVERPOOL CANAL, BOOTLE: After the Friday broadcast I went up to Bootle to see the stretch of canal bank which Kevin McNulty and team had been landscaping (see 23 March). I easily found it because of the concentration of ducks, swans and Coots! This local and private initiative is of great value as an example to others of what can be done to improve the local environment. I found 18 species of birds along the canal, including Grey Wagtails and Sparrowhawk with a family of Dabchicks a little further on, almost certainly the nearest to the Pier Head less than three miles away.

22 SEPTEMBER: FIRST REDWINGS OF THE WINTER IN FAZAKERLEY: When I was out along Higher Lane today I was amazed to find four Redwings, much earlier than usual. There also seemed to be a lot of Song Thrushes and Blackbirds about – mainly on elderberries. The weather situation had been favourable for an arrival of winter visitors from Scandinavia: a depression over the North Sea with strong E/NE winds.   Adrian Leigh

**SUNDAY 23 SEPT:
MERSEY TUNNEL 10K
ROAD RACE TO NEW
BRIGHTON**

Seacombe Ferry Terminal

As we crossed from the Pier Head to Seacombe on the ten o'clock ferry we looked for the hundreds of people running through the tunnel directly below us – in aid of the Royal Liverpool Children's Hospital League of Friends. We didn't see them of course – until they emerged and ran past us at the Seacombe Ferry terminal where we were able to see what really lurks beneath the Mersey by visiting the aquarium.

A wonderful surprise on the grass outside: a Painted Lady (butterfly!), only a few reported this year. Black Medick caught our eye, also Black Nightshade, Wild Pansy still in flower and a giant Silverfish, one of the many which crawl and jump along the seawall. Lots of fossils in the limestone boulders. Marvellous views of at least 300 Turnstones, 100 Redshanks and 25 Ringed Plovers roosting the tide on the breakwater.

A pair of Mute Swans flew low along the prom – always a wonderful sight. Noisy Grey Wagtails alerted us to a Sparrowhawk dashing towards the trees of Vale Park and a late Spotted Flycatcher by Guinea Gap Baths.

28 SEPTEMBER: PIER HEAD TO PARADISE (STREET) NATURE TRAIL: Robins everywhere. One in the dark on Derby Square, one around the *Edmund Gardner* pilot boat where Grey Wagtails were very active, probably three, along with a Pied Wagtail, all wanting to feed down in the graving dock. A (migrating?) Red Admiral flew along the Pier Head.

RARE NEWTS MADE HOMELESS IN WALLASEY: I reported on my visit to a pond in Breck Road, Wallasey, where the discovery of Great Crested Newts, protected by European laws, had held up a major building project. The builders now had the special licence they needed which allowed newts to be moved to a new home if they stood in the way of a project which was in the overriding public interest and when no alternative was available. However neither of these conditions seemed to apply because alternative sites had been considered for the school and were still available.

SUNDAY 30 SEPT: LIVERPOOL LOOP LINE WALTON HALL PARK
RICE LANE CITY FARM

Mallow, Evening Primrose, giant Sun Spurges, Prickly Sowthistle, Knapweed, Bramble, Hairy Tare, Black Medick, Red Bartsia, Yellow Melilot, Ragwort, Wild Radish, Horse Mint, Bladder Campion, Yarrow, Black Nightshade, Feverfew and Persicaria were amongst the wayside flowers we found just round the corner from Rice Lane Station and along the Loop Line by Hartley's Village. Fine views of a Sparrowhawk which put up a large flock of Starlings. Robins ticking and singing, a flock of Goldfinches, a noisy group of Long Tailed Tits in the poplars by the Seven Sisters fishing pond where the only angler we saw was a Heron.

Another highlight of the day was the unexpected blue sky and strong wind gusting through the trees ripping off flurries of leaves. Canada Geese, Mallard and Coot on the lake in Walton Hall Park (no sign of the Great Crested Grebes which have been nesting there). Plenty of exotic animals en route too: a huge 'ram' in the 'children's zoo' and lots more at Rice Lane City Farm on the site of Walton cemetery just across the road from the gaol - which we decided not to visit!

THE MOTHS OF SEFTON PARK: During my job I come across many dead moths each day and always admire the different colours and shapes. So far I have identified 20 species, including three Red Underwings which the books say is very rare to the north. Other moths: Eyed Hawkmoth, White Ermine, Common Footman, Four Spot Footman, Scalloped Oak, Heart and Dart, Mother of Pearl, Foxglove Pug, Scarce Silverlines, Large Yellow Underwing, Swallowtail, Lilac Beauty, Vapourer Moth, Angle Shades, Garden Carpet, Orange Underwing, Herald, Barred Yellow.

Alan McGlynn

Our BBC Radio Merseyside Nature Watch concentrates on things which are easy to find, for all to see. But Alan's report shows just how much is going on out there that we don't usually see. The wonderful names create the impression that there is a completely different, unknown world right on our very doorsteps. We don't have to go out looking for UFOs. Plenty of UFOs in your own back garden!

BUZZARDS IN RUNCORN…I have noticed a group of Buzzards, two adults and three young ones, flying over open farmland and woodland. The young Buzzards fly very high together. I have been told that the Buzzards have been returning in May/June for about three years now.   Bob Hughes (not me, my namesake!)

…AND IN AIGBURTH: I have seen a Buzzard over the Aigburth-Sefton Park area several times now.   Robin Surtees

HEDGEHOGS IN THE CITY CENTRE: I have seen quite a few squashed Hedgehogs on the road this summer. The nearest to the city centre was at the corner of New Islington and Norton Street.   Joe Kennedy

30 SEPTEMBER: NATURE WATCH NEWS

The weather situation has had a major effect on bird movements and sightings during the last two weeks. A depression over the North Sea meant easterly winds from Scandinavia and northerly winds from Iceland. As a result several rare Sabine's Gulls from the high Arctic were seen – from Crosby to Leasowe. Wigeon and Pintail duck arrived on the Mersey and Dee marshes from distant breeding grounds. Martin Mere has already had 10000 Pinkfooted Geese from Iceland, earlier than usual because of the favourable winds which also brought early winter Redwings – four at Fazakerley on 22 Sept and a few others reported since. Not only Redwings: an influx of Yellow Browed Warblers has been reported, one joining a party of Long Tailed Tits also in Fazakerley. They come from Siberia/northern Asia.

On a more local scale there was a 'rush' of Meadow Pipits on the pleasant morning of 26 Sept after small numbers had been seen or heard passing over Merseyside since 14 Sept. Still more to come and look out for Skylarks, Chaffinches and other 'partial migrants' passing over in the coming weeks. Jays, Woodpeckers and Squirrels are moving around, often coming into gardens now. Snipe on marshy ground since 20 Sept. Robins – and Grey Wagtails seem to be 'everywhere' at the moment.

A few Swallows and House Martins are still with us, also Blackcaps and Chiffchaffs, but no Reed Warblers for over two weeks and probably a last Whitethroat skulking in brambles on 20 Sept. Two late Spotted Flycatchers on 22 Sept, another on 23rd. The last two weeks of September and early October are usually the best time to see Mute Swans in flight – a wonderful sight – and noise from their wings! They are moving away from nesting sites looking for suitable winter quarters including park lakes where they know they will be fed. One which arrived at Central Park, Wallasey had a white ring ABHJ - probably from North Wales (green rings are usually birds from South Lancs/Cheshire; blue rings may be Shropshire or further afield so please report).

News of a third pair of Peregrines nesting at a 'secret' location but within 'striking distance' of the Pier Head. A Raven back at the Anglican Cathedral on 13 Sept. Regular sightings of Buzzards around Runcorn suggest they are now nesting there as well as in Wirral and Knowsley, so Merseyside is now surrounded by Buzzards which can't really be expected to come any closer. But you never know!....

The weather had a big effect on the butterflies as well as the birds. Hardly any seen on the wet or cool days 15-19 Sept but 20 Sept was sunny, almost humid for a few hours when I saw a 'record' 12 Red Admirals on a short stretch of Michaelmas Daisies. Small Tortoiseshells were also abundant but have since been dropping off again (literally?!). One Comma then four on 24 Sept – another fine day – and 20 Sept was also the day when I saw my last Common Blues, both tired and worn. Whites, Speckled Woods and Small Copper still flying at the end of the month, also Silver-Y moths on Michaelmas Daisies (Michaelmas Day = 29 Sept!). Bats still flying on 28 Sept. Spiders webs glistening damp. Leaves starting to carpet the ground. Autumn. Enjoy it!

4 OCTOBER: SEFTON PARK: Tawny Owls have been very vocal the last few weeks. Foxes – as many as three together – seen regularly and another Grey Squirrel – still quite uncommon in the park. Alan McGlynn

I was surprised to see about 60 Canada Geese on the lake in Sefton Park – in two 'rival' groups – new arrivals I think. Wilf Murray

On 19 October I counted two groups totalling 86 and another 25 in Greenbank Park – a further winter increase.

5 OCTOBER: PIER HEAD TO PARADISE (STREET) NATURE TRAIL: Gusty showers and rain. About 100 gulls on Chavasse Park until disturbed by first passers-by. Wren singing. A female Blackbird very tame and acting dazed – probably just escaped a Sparrowhawk attack judging by the state of its tail. Only two Robins after last week's 'rush'. A Grey Wagtail feeding along the side of Canning Dock by the Strand. A Cormorant on Salthouse Dock – dives lasting about 30 seconds. I took a Chavasse Park apple back to the studio and some Ivy now in flower, but I had the impression that Morning Merseyside's Andy Ball had been more excited about the Hops which I had taken in a week or two before – from the site of an old pub in Wallasey, long since pulled down!

OUTRAGE OVER TREE FELLING IN THINGWALL, Wirral: I reported on my visit to see a plot of land in Pensby Road where trees, mainly chestnuts, had been felled to make way for a new 'development'. On checking with the planning department, the Land Registry Office and Gavin Weir, Wirral's tree preservation officer, we were told that it was not illegal to remove trees on private property unless they had a special preservation order.

WATER VOLES GIVE NETHERLEY A BOOST: After Friday's broadcast I went out to see Gladys and Billy Lea, regular Nature Watch listeners who had described themselves as a couple of recycled teenagers which I found to be very much the case! They were able to tell me that Water Voles had been found on Netherley Brook which was now going to be cleaned up as a special conservation area. Water Voles helping the community to a better environment! They had also seen Kingfishers on the brook and I found 30 species of birds in the area, including my last Swallows for the year, four Yellowhammers and a Buzzard over by the M62!

6 OCT: STONEYCROFT: Thank you for your tips on butterfly plants. We had a visit from a Comma on 1 Oct – the only one this year, a fine specimen. We've had Michaelmas Daisies in the garden but the butterflies have not gone on them. When we had large numbers of Painted Ladies (1966?) I noticed they preferred the white buddleia to the purple buddleia. Is there also a painted man butterfly? And a manbird to go with a ladybird? Fiona and Chris Marsden

Three interesting stories here: I've had several confirmations that butterflies love Michaelmas Daisies growing wild, but not in gardens. Why? On 21 Sept on the canal in Bootle I had seen four Red Admirals going quite wild about a small white buddleia ignoring the more prolific purple. Why? And in Nature Watch News I had suggested that a female Emperor Moth should be called an Empress. Why not?!

88

SUNDAY 7 OCT: A KILLER WHALE -   AT THE WIRRAL BUS AND TRAM SHOW !

Field sketch of what we saw

It was the Wirral Bus and Tram Show that had taken us to Woodside to end up in exactly the right place at exactly the right time to see the first ever Killer Whale that had come into the Mersey!

The trip to Woodside began at the Pier Head and we were met by more BBC Radio Merseyside Nature Watchers when we got off the ferry, watched closely by the local feral pigeons. On a walk along the front towards Cammell Laird's we saw a shrubbery with many trees and shrubs, some cultivated, others naturalised.

Walking back towards Woodside Ferry the group became transfixed by the huge dorsal fin of a whale. The enormous mammal had seemingly arrived on the incoming tide and was heading steadily towards Widnes.

After we regained our senses we passed through Pacific Road where there were many old buses and coaches on display The smoke bellowing out of the miniature steam engines was in complete contrast to the pollutants expired from our more modern forms of transport.

As we passed roadside verges and 'wasteland' we discovered buddleja davidii still in flower and Purple Toadflax (Linaria purpurea). The name 'toadflax' originates from the open flower's resemblance to a toad's mouth and the plant's similarity to flax – used in herb medicine for healing jaundice or steeped in milk to make fly poison. Wild Mignonette, a plant of calcareous soils, was growing close to the docks.

We encountered many species of birds on our way to from Woodside to Seacombe with both Grey and Pied Wagtails, a flock of agitated Redshank at Morpeth Dock close to the Peregrine's nest site (!), Oystercatcher, gulls, Cormorants and the Great Crested Grebe on the dock by Tower Quays.

All I can say is – we had a whale of a time !   Tony Whewell

Tony was too modest to say that he was the first to spot the Killer Whale. The rest of us would certainly have walked on obliviously if Tony hadn't seen it and shouted to us. (How he spots a whale in the river when he's delving into bushes remains a mystery!)

7 OCTOBER: BBC RADIO MERSEYSIDE NATURE WATCH WAS THERE….

Extracts from eye witness accounts of the first ever sighting of a Killer Whale in the Mersey:

Tony and myself were lagging behind the rest of the group looking at a locust tree when Tony pointed out to the river and said something like: ' Oh my god, is that what I think it is?!' There, heading up the river on the tide, was this huge black dorsal fin which then disappeared below the waves. It was only when it reappeared that I was convinced of what we were seeing.   Joe Ellis, Netherton.

Could Tony possibly be saying that he had seen a whale? Surely not. A whale? On the Mersey? You must be joking! Quickly raising my binoculars I scanned the waters and yes, there it was, an impressive fin breaking the surface and then disappearing making steady progress upstream.

Mick Washington and Betty Griffiths, West Kirby

As we stood in astonishment, not really believing our eyes, the fin sheared through the water, then disappeared beneath the surface.   Margaret Parry, Stoneycroft

The group members, while trying not to lose their composure at such a tremendous sight, could not help but lose control of their lower jaws as we all gaped in wonder.

Tony Whewell, Crosby

We were close to Cammell Laird, Priory Wharf, when the shout went up: Whale! After whale watching in Alaska and Teneriffe this was happening on the banks of the Mersey! Could I believe my eyes? Could I not!

Julia Yeardsley, Bromborough

We had just left Woodside Ferry at 11.30. I was serving in the cafeteria on the 'Woodchurch'. When I looked up I saw something in the river between us and Cammell Laird's. It was the huge fin of a whale. When we turned back towards the Pier Head, the whale was still heading up the river. Scott, one of the deck hands, saw it too.   Vicky Ellis, Mersey Ferries

I was walking in Pickering's Pasture, Hale with my partner. She suddenly said: what's that out there? It looks like a shark or something. I laughed and said don't be daft, but when I looked myself I saw that it was more than a shark! It could only be a whale coasting up the river on a fast tide at about 3 p.m.. It was diving and coming to the surface so we presume it was still alive. When we got back to the car we heard about it on BBC Radio Merseyside. Somebody else had seen it at Otterspool.

Gordon Roberts, Speke

.... THE FIRST EVER KILLER WHALE TO COME INTO THE MERSEY

Woodside Ferry

The only other record of a Killer Whale that we could find was of one beached at West Kirby on 22 March 1876, bought by a Peter Lunt and chopped up for 'blubber and oil', as reported by Thomas J. Moore in the proceedings of the Liverpool Literary and Philosophical Society on 17 April 1876. So this was indeed the first Killer Whale ever to be seen in the Mersey and first spotted, it seemed, by our Sunday Nature Watch team. In the last two or three years only 7 or 8 had been seen anywhere around the British Isles. Earlier in the year a pair of Killer Whales with a youngster swam into Cork harbour. The female died of blood poisoning from a broken tooth, which just goes to show that whales can be ill and disorientated for quite simple, though unexpected reasons. The books said that an estimated 1,500 Killer Whales live around Iceland and Norway, total 'European' population 4,000-10,000.

It seemed almost certain that the whale would end up stranded somewhere – like Bottle Nosed Whales and Pilot Whales in the past – most likely off Speke or Hale.

When the tide goes out on the Mersey it is like pulling the plug out of the bath which would leave a whale high and dry. All we could do was wait and see.

TUESDAY 9 OCTOBER: DEAD ON SANDBANK: Julia Yeardsley at BBC Radio Merseyside who had also been with us on the Sunday telephoned me to say that the airport had reported the Killer Whale dead on a sandbank out in the river. That evening BBC's Northwest Tonight with Gordon Burns showed pictures of the whale lying on its side with one flipper up in the air.

WEDNESDAY 10 OCTOBER: I went down to see the whale after hearing the news on yesterday's Northwest Tonight. There were a lot of people there and it was sad to see that the whale had come to such a tragic end. Gordon Roberts

RPSCA chief inspector Martin Marsh went out by helicopter to examine the whale, which was 15 feet in length. There was blood coming from the blow hole, normally a sign of stress or lung injuries, though it had looked very strong and alive when we had seen it on the Sunday.

FRIDAY 12 OCTOBER: The RSPCA informed the Maritime Mammals Stranding Project in London and Paul Jepson came up to examine the whale. Skin samples were taken away for DNA tests from which it might be possible to establish where the whale had come from.

Courtesy Liverpool Daily Post & Echo

Roland Parkes, RSPCA

SUNDAY 14 OCTOBER: INSHORE RESCUE INCIDENT REPORT:

Time alerted: 14.00   *Station initiating: HM Coastguard*

Weather: E-SE 5   MIST   MOD VIS   Tide: HW 10.01 8.8m LW 16.33 1.8m

Incident details: Member of the public reported a large object in the water off Cammell Laird – asked to investigate by Coastguard.

On arrival object was seen to be the Orca Whale carcass (i.e. Killer Whale – Orca orcina). Whale was marked with a high vis marker buoy (orange) weighted down with a length of chain, last seen heading north from Egg (i.e. the buoy off Egremont).

Casualty details: one large, very smelly Orca Whale.

Andrew Fell, Inshore Rescue, Pier Head

TUESDAY 16 OCTOBER: HM COASTGUARD INCIDENT REPORT:

At 15.30 we received a report from Sefton rangers that the whale had been washed up on Crosby beach 100 metres south of Mariner's Road.

Paul Sutton, HM Coastguard

The whale was cut up on the beach and taken away to be disposed of, probably incinerated.

Paul Wisse, Sefton Council

SAVE THE WHALE: It is a shame it wasn't possible to catch up with the whale somehow and guide it back out of the river before it became stranded and died.

Kathy Andrews, Garston

14 OCT : NATURE WATCH NEWS

The sensation of the last two weeks - the year, the century?! – was, of course, the Killer Whale spotted by our Sunday Nature Watch team on 7 Oct at Woodside and dealt with in detail elsewhere.

No reports of summer birds since 5 Oct when 14 Swallows, 4 House Martins and a 'Willowchiff' – probably a Chiffchaff were reported. Any since? Fair numbers of Meadow Pipits have continued to pass over on favourable days (since ca 15 Sept) and Skylarks noted since around 6 Oct in increasing numbers. Flocks of Mistle Thrushes totalling 35 birds over Birkenhead docks on 3 Oct ('trrrk' calls). No Fieldfares reported yet ('chack,chack') but a flock of 18 Redwings at Knotty Ash on 14 Oct. Listen out for them passing over your house at night in the coming weeks: a high pitched drawn out 'tseeep'. Big movement of Chaffinches and Meadow Pipits over the Pier Head at first light on 12 Oct – also Skylarks, Woodpigeons, Rooks and Jackdaws.

Pied Wagtails have been seen in quite large numbers in many places: over 30 on a field in Netherley on 5 Oct; six on the cricket pitch, Central Park, Wallasey next day etc. Grey Wagtails also still very conspicuous. And Robins: probably another new influx on 12 Oct. Hedge Sparrows also conspicuous again with some song on 4-7 Oct. Like Robins and most other small birds they evacuate Scandinavia and eastern Europe for the winter, so presumably there is an influx of continental Hedge Sparrows too, though little attention seems to have been paid to them by ornithologists. Magpies have been using communal roosts again since the end of Sept in growing numbers. Is there a roost near you? And where are Rooks and Jackdaws roosting? Please report roosts and flight lines to and from them.

The Swan – ring ABHJ – which I reported in the last Nature Watch News as an example of how Mute Swans pass through Merseyside from nesting sites to winter haunts was ringed as a cygnet near Llandudno in 1998 and had never been away from the North Wales coast until it turned up in Central Park, Wallasey on 29 Sept – gone next day, probably chased off (or on?!) by another unringed Swan.

After a report of five Buzzards – a family – seen regularly around Runcorn, five were seen crossing the Mersey at Frodsham around the same time as one was seen by the M62 at Huyton-Childwall. Four Yellowhammers together in the fields there around Tarbock. Water Voles have been found on Netherley Brook which is now being cleaned up as a special conservation area. Good news, bad news: the head of one of the Fazakerley badgers was found in Bluebell Woods. The 'overwhelming' number of Sparrowhawks reported this year must be a major factor in the sparrow decline. A Mediterranean Gull was at Marine Lake, New Brighton on 10 Oct – like a Blackheaded Gull but 'pure white all over'. If it is still there look for it on the rain puddle on the site of old New Brighton baths where it went – yes – to bathe!

Eight species of butterflies still flying 11-12 Oct, Small and Large White, Tortoiseshells, Red Admiral, Comma and Speckled Wood and Small Copper– all still looking 'strong' and even a Peacock which must have come back out of hibernation in the warm weather on 8 and 11 Oct (last reported 6 Sept!).

SUNDAY 14 OCTOBER : THE JAM BUTTY MINES OF KNOTTY ASH

Comedian Ken Dodd created his own history – and geography – of Knotty Ash so we decided to go in search of the famous Jam Butty Mines – or at least the fruits of autumn which provided the raw materials for the jam! We didn't find them in the Little Bongs – a lovely secluded terrace off the main street (begging the question from one of the group: where are the Big Bongs!) . However along the Loop Line we discovered an old railway tunnel, partly blocked, which was clearly a relic of the underground fruit machines. Fluffy Hemp Agrimony had obviously been the inspiration for the famous tickling stick but it was Japanese Anemones that we found growing in Doddy's diddy garden. At St John's church we bumped into Paul the sexton who denied they had bats in the belfry, only pigeons. But he did show us a grave slab under which was the home (or 'resting place' as one aspiring comedian in the group put it) of a hedgehog, which often got stuck in a sunken grave and had to be helped out. By about one o'clock we were eating our own jam butties, specially provided, in the imaginary shade of the original knotty ash tree which had been a landmark on the road from Prescot to Liverpool (i.e. the Knotty Ash pub!).   A Sparrowhawk flew over with a Magpie on its tail. Earlier a flock of 18 Redwings had flown out of Springfield Park. Grey Wagtails were on the roof of the community centre and a further exploration of the Loop Line towards Sandfield Park produced a Grey Squirrel, Great Spotted Woodpecker, Jay, Long Tailed Tits and a great variety of fungusses, as Ken Dodd would no doubt also spell it! There IS something special about Knotty Ash. Everybody felt quite enchanted. Something they put in the jam?!

19 OCTOBER: BIG MIGRATION DAY FOR BIRDS -AND BUTTERFLIES!

PIER HEAD TO PARADISE (STREET) NATURE TRAIL: Big movement of migrants. Over 200 Fieldfares in seven flocks in about 20 minutes, two smaller groups of Redwings; Chaffinches, Meadow Pipits, Pied Wagtails.

WAVERTREE PLAYGROUND: More Redwings, Fieldfares, Chaffinches and Skylarks over the 'Mystery' and over FALLOWFIELD ROAD as I made my way to see Margaret Thompson, a regular Nature Watch listener and contributor. Margaret is very much housebound and had impressed me with the detail - and humour -of her observations from an upstairs window which I was able to see for myself.

HALE HEAD: The number of Fieldfares and Redwings passing over in the direction of Frodsham must have been in the thousands. They were coming at different heights, high and low, a lot of them landing in the fields to feed or rest. I also had the wonderful experience of watching a Peregrine stoop at one of the flocks.

Tony Craven

HIGHTOWN: I was fascinated to see dozens of Red Admirals heading out across the sea in the direction of Leasowe lighthouse.   David Bryant

HILBRE ISLAND: As well as birds passing overhead at least 200 migrating Red Admirals came in off the sea – an amazing sight and quite late in the year for such migration.   Jeff Clarke

SUNDAY 21 OCTOBER: PIER HEAD MIGRATION WATCH

Killer Whale award ceremony at the Pier Head. Bob the Birdman (left) with Tony Whewell

No migration to watch! It was quiet after the 'rush' of birds that had been seen on the Friday. No signs of migration either at Seaforth or Hale, perhaps because there was now a north wind rather than S/SE. But we still had a great day out. I told the group about the busy programme there had been at and around the Pier Head the day before:

FOOD FOR FREE: Lots of free samples at the Liverpool Food Festival at the Pier Head with BBC Radio Merseyside chef Tom Bridge on board the *'Royal Daffodil'*.

A YEAR IN THE WILDLIFE OF CHESHIRE AND WIRRAL: A meeting of the Merseyside Naturalists' Association (MNA) at the Bluecoat (also on our Pier Head to Paradise –Street- Nature Trail!). An excellent talk with slides by Wirral ranger Jeff Clarke. (200 species of moths in a Widnes garden!)

HOW GREEN IS YOUR LIFE? Several BBC Radio Merseyside Nature Watch listeners attended the seminar organised by the Centre for Sustainable Living at Manor Trust, Gorsey Lane, Wallasey, chaired by Professor Tony Bradshaw, a prominent figure in environmental circles on Merseyside and much further afield. Composting; Recycling; Energy Efficiency; Green Transport.

PRINCES DOCK: Then we explored the 'new' Princes Dock area where a flock of about 50 Linnets was feeding on some bare ground. New Zealand 'hebe', Sea Pink and Rosemary had been planted in a bed of 'slate mulch' by the new buildings where we saved a big sleepy Bumble Bee by returning it to the 'flower bed'! A young Swan on Princes Half Tide Dock was probably one of the Clarence Dock cygnets.

KILLER WHALE AWARD: Mirth and merriment as we made a very formal presentation of a statuette of a Killer Whale (a little toy rubber one!) to whale spotter extraordinaire Tony Whewell on the podium in front of the Liver Buildings. Then into the ferry terminal for a 'picnic', a chat and a much appreciated warm-up!

TWO KILLER WHALES OFF ANGLESEY – IN 1965: I received the following message from Hull: *On 25 June 1965 I saw two Killer Whales from the pilot boat off Moelfre, Anglesey. Very close views of one: high dorsal fin, white face patch, large size.*   Ray Eades, Retired Liverpool River Pilot

SUNDAY 28 OCTOBER : AUTUMN LEAVES IN NEWSHAM PARK

"The time is probably not very far distant when there will be nothing green, save Newsham Park, between the Old Swan and the river."   Liverpool Review 1884

A glorious sunny autumn day. We met outside the abattoir in Prescot Road – an unlikely place for a Sunday Nature Watch! But we were soon round the corner away from the noise of the traffic watching a Jay flying over and a Great Spotted Woodpecker investigating a poplar tree. A flock of about 20 migrating Jackdaws and two Rooks flew over to the west, a Fieldfare and a couple of Skylarks. The big surprise was to find as many as 22 Mute Swans packed onto the relatively small boating lake – recent arrivals, we were told by locals. Two were ringed (later we heard one was from Warrington, one from Chester), one had a fishing hook stuck in its leg. We informed the rangers – unfortunately hooks and twine are a very common problem. Also about 70 Canada Geese and nice to see a pair of Pochard amongst the Mallard, Moorhens and Coots. It was difficult to believe we were in the middle of Liverpool – not a house in view except the magnificent buildings and tower of the old orphanage.

LISTER DRIVE WILD FLOWER MEADOW: Over the railway from the park. The notice said: "A haven for wild flowers, birds, butterflies, bees and other wildlife. It was created with the help of local children on the site of an old (Manweb) power station and is now an open air classroom."

LISTER DRIVE BATHS TAKEN OVER BY FISH: Sounds logical enough! I could just imagine how the idea to convert the baths into a 'fish farm' had come about – in typical Scouse fashion: The baths are closing down? Great, I could put all my fish in there! It reminded me of an aquatic version of Quiggins 'Old Curiosity Shop' in College Lane just round the corner from BBC Radio Merseyside – another Merseyside 'must be seen to be believed'! However, the longer we stayed looking at the other pets – rabbits, guinea pigs, parrots, tropical fish, even newts – the sadder we felt, seeing the 'impersonal' side of the large scale pet industry.

BUZZARD OVER OLD SWAN: And just to finish off with, a Buzzard appeared quite low over Old Swan coming from the direction of Knowsley, possibly heading for the Anglican Cathedral as a landmark on its way across the Mersey to an unknown destination.

28 OCTOBER: FRESHFIELD: Lots of flowers still out – White Campion, Evening Primrose, Centaury, Hawkweed, Ragwort, Common Storksbill. No butterflies but we did see several small red dragonflies (or are they darters?). In the pinewoods were several fungi, including a type of russula, honey fungus and puffball – and lots of others unidentified.   Margaret Parry

29 OCTOBER: JAYS AND WOODPECKERS MOVE INTO WALLASEY: I had never seen Jays or Great Spotted Woodpeckers on the Wallasey side of the docks before, not in 40-50 years. But this autumn both species were 'caught in the act' of crossing from the trees which have recently been planted on the old Bidston Moss rubbish tip which now form a green 'bridge' into Wallasey from Bidston Hill. Coal Tits have also started to turn up. Nuthatches and Tree Creepers to follow?!

31 OCTOBER : NATURE WATCH NEWS

The story of the Killer Whale dominated the Nature Watch headlines for most of October! Here a final summary:

After the Killer Whale was spotted by our Sunday Nature Watch group at Woodside at 11.30 on 7 Oct it was seen off Hale Head about 15.00 (just on high tide) still swimming and diving. On Tuesday 9 Oct it was dead on a sandbank off Speke. After DNA samples had been taken – in the hope of establishing where the whale had come from – the corpse was abandoned to its fate – too difficult (or too costly?) to secure. The inshore rescue team was alerted on Sunday 14 Oct when the carcass of the whale was spotted off Cammell Laird's. They put an orange marker buoy on the whale and 'escorted' it to the mouth of the river as it floated out on the tide. On Tuesday 16 Oct it was finally washed up on Crosby shore where it was cut up to be disposed of – very smelly and decaying by this time. A sad end to such a magnificent creature.

In the last Nature Watch News I wrote of a 'late' autumn but it's been more like a second spring! The warmest October on record (since 1659). One of the effects was a freshly hatched Meadow Brown butterfly on 18 Oct – usually finished early Sept. The late flying butterflies are later than ever: Red Admiral, Small Tortoiseshell, Comma and Small Copper all still flying on 27 Oct. But also Speckled Wood and Small White. One of my two remaining Large White cocoons was empty, butterfly flown, probably also on 27 Oct.

Strange things happening in the garden too: I saw a (young) laburnum with a fresh bloom and lilac with small new purple spikes. As well as the usual late flowers such as Michaelmas Daisies, Ragwort, Yarrow, Hawkbit, I found Common Vetch, Herb Robert, Hop Clover amongst those coming back into flower. Please report ALL flowers seen out in November!

19 Oct was a big migration day: Fieldfares and Redwings seen passing over in many places including the Pier Head, Wavertree Playground, Hale Head. Not only birds: migrating Red Admirals were seen heading out to sea at Hightown and at least 200 coming in from the sea at Hilbre Island . A Firecrest at Warbreck Moor, Aintree, reflected a widespread influx – 15 reported on Bardsey Island at the same time.

The last Swallows of the year to be reported appear to have been those seen by BBC Radio Merseyside's Andy Ball on his canal trip 6-11 Oct though I hear a few more were seen through to the end of the month. Great Spotted Woodpecker, Jay and Coal Tit have all turned up in Wallasey for the first time this October – a direct result of the trees planted on the old Bidston Moss rubbish tip creating a green 'bridge' across to Wallasey from Bidston Hill. 152 pairs of Buzzards nesting in Cheshire! That is from about ten pairs only five years ago in 1994 – simply unbelievable! Short Eared Owls are now hunting in several places including the Dee marshes. Polecats have been moving into Cheshire from North Wales with strongholds in 'inaccessible' places such as Stanlow – some seen squashed on the motorway there. The young Peregrine which fell into the ventilation shaft at Woodside in June is still at Thurstaston Country Park recovering from its ordeal.

1 NOVEMBER: RICE LANE CITY FARM (see Sunday Nature Watch 30 Sept) featured on BBC TV's Northwest Tonight as an example of where the money goes to from BBC's Children in Need Appeal (this year on 16 November).

2 NOVEMBER: PIER HEAD TO PARADISE (STREET) NATURE TRAIL: I had already found 40 species of wild flowers still showing colour in this mild autumn and on my walk around Chavasse Park I found 15 different kinds still in flower, including our speciality – Yellow Balsam. A posie of flowers for Linda McDermott and some Chavasse Park champignons for Andy Ball!

THE MOLE OF EDGE HILL: No, not a speciality of the local fauna – I'd hoped to track it down on our visit to Newsham Park until they told me it was the nickname of Joseph Williamson who kept his unemployed workers busy digging tunnels – just for fun so to speak! (But we did find the pub of the same name!). The Friends of the Williamson Tunnels organise visits, well worth seeing - and hearing the fascinating story.

GRUBBY LAWNS IN HESWALL: The Mole of Edge Hill had nothing to do with the lawns which were mysteriously being dug up on the other side of the river. I went out to investigate. I first found patches of grass dug up at the junction of Telegraph Road and Thurstaston Road. It looked like the work of foxes, possibly badgers, but I couldn't find any tell tale footprints. Just down Thurstaston Road the grass at Dawstone Court was in a terrible state. Lawn specialist Stephen Coathup said that they were after cockchafer grubs, a problem which had occurred here only in the last two or three years though it was a regular problem down south. I did some grubbing about myself but couldn't find any grubs! But I did notice that the soil was very light and sandy and the grass of very good quality. One to watch out for in future, perhaps.

BARN OWLS - AND UFOs! - IN HUYTON: On Sunday night (28 Oct) I was intrigued by a bright 'headlight' in the sky to the west. I went out into the garden to get a better view. Whatever it was I don't know but I was rewarded with the sight of a Barn Owl flying low along the roof tops looking down into gardens by the M62.

Tony Craven

YELLOWHAMMER AWARD: I had gone out to see Tony to give him the promised reward for being the first to report a Yellowhammer within 5-10 miles of the Pier Head – at Tarbock. Ever since I had cheekily claimed the reward myself (see 8 Aug) I had had a bad conscience, so I gave Tony a bottle of *Rondone Rosso* (Red Swift – my 'concoction!') – not to be opened until the first Swifts return next spring.

WELL TRAVELLED GOOSE IN CENTRAL PARK, Wallasey: The Canada Goose which you reported spending at least the last two years in Central Park was ringed (white CVA) as an adult female at Angram near York in 1992 so she is at least ten years old. In summer 1994 and 1995 she was seen at the popular moulting grounds at the Beauly Firth, Inverness, 280 miles to the north and was then not reported again until you contacted us. Many thanks.

Andy Baxter, Central Science Laboratory (DEFRA), York

SUNDAY 4 NOV: AUTUMN LEAVES – DIBBINSDALE TO THE MERSEY SHORE

Still Life? Autumn leaves with welly boot.
Photo : Val Curtis

The timing was spot on. At one point we were caught in a shower of leaves falling down upon us like snow as we looked at the Otter's Tunnel, home to many bats – Pipistrelle, Daubenton's, Noctule. A beautiful golden carpet of leaves under a group of beech trees and later we were kicking up leaves along Bromborough Road (specially closed off for us ?!).

A couple of Teal were on the flooded field and a Heron flew over. Four-year-old Robert was the hero of the day. He earned a round of applause for nonchalantly identifying a tree as an oak tree – not even an acorn tree as many children would say. He also found Reindeer Horn Tree – a sapling – and Birds Wing Ferns! A Red Admiral came and joined us for a while at Woodslee Pond and at the visitors centre we were very lucky to bump into Pete the ranger who told us about his recent trip to Iceland – home of the many Pinkfooted Geese and Whooper Swans now arriving in the Merseyside region. He then showed us round the 'secret' walled garden with its various composting systems (including redworms!) and took us down to his 'natural' bird feeding station – a clearing in the woods.

The group was not disappointed with the surprise views of the Mersey which I had promised – another new angle on Liverpool – reached by a route which we all promised to keep secret!

5 NOVEMBER: BONFIRE NIGHT: How on earth do the birds cope with all the fireworks on Bonfire Night, before and after? My animals are still frightend. The cat is a nervous wreck.   Dorothy Jones, Huyton (20 Nov)

6 NOVEMBER: TWO-DAY CLEAN UP IN BIRKENHEAD PARK: BBC Radio Merseyside's Claire Evans was in the park where Rangers and RSPCA were about to clear litter and fishing twine from the park lakes. On 28 Oct in Newsham Park we had seen a Swan with a hook in its leg and I've seen many Canada Geese around Merseyside's parks limping with twine wrapped tightly round their legs. The RSPCA had been called out 170 times this year - to Birkenhead Park alone!

6 NOVEMBER: SALMON RETURN TO THE MERSEY: 'Morning Merseyside' also reported on the Environment Agency's discovery of migrating Salmon above Woolston Weir at Warrington – one of the two was 3ft long and weighed 15lb. There had been several stories about Salmon in the river, cleaner now than at any time in the last 200 years, but this was the first 'official' proof.

MORE SIGNS OF A CLEANER MERSEY: I caught up with Andrew Fell at last, the inshore rescue officer who had escorted the carcass of the Killer Whale out of the river on 14 October. He was sure that they had seen Salmon in the river for some time already but he also told me of more subtle signs that the river was now much cleaner. It was only in the last couple of years that the build up of algae and barnacles on their rescue boats had to be cleaned off every two weeks. The growth could reduce the speed of the boats from a maximum of 42 knots to 34 knots!

SEALS AT THE PIER HEAD... Andrew also told me that they had regular sightings of Grey Seals in the river. Early mornings they had even come into the 'lagoon' behind the landing stage. Terry, security guard at Clarence Dock had told us earlier in the year that he had seen a seal from the ferry soon after leaving the Pier Head and the ferry crew told me they saw them too, most often around Seacombe in winter. Perhaps this had something to do with the same shoals of fish which the Great Crested Grebes fished just inside the docks from Seacombe on Alfred Dock and the East Float (Mullet?).

...AND KINGFISHERS! Not this year but Andrew remembered watching a beautiful Kingfisher fishing from the chains which secure the landing stage at the Pier Head. In 1985 a Kingfisher flew into a window of the Maritime Museum at Albert Dock.

DECAPITATED DOLPHIN – VICTIM OF THE KILLER WHALE? Inshore Rescue had also recovered a headless six-foot Dolphin. Normally such finds would be attributed to damage from a ship's propeller screw. But the 'bite' was too clean suggesting indeed the bite of a Killer Whale – the one which came into the river a few weeks later? Had they already met up somewhere out at sea and both ended up in the Mersey on different tides?

THE LOST ROOKS OF SEFTON: There used to be a large rookery in huge old trees surrounding the old vicarage near Sefton church until the early 1970s.

Shirley Hudson.

I went out to see Shirley 'for old time's sake'. I knew the Sefton rookery from the 1960s when I had made a survey of Rooks and rookeries – on the Wirral side of the river! In winter the Sefton Rooks used to fly right across the whole of built up Merseyside (ca 15 miles) to a roost in Arrowe Park. They used to cross the Mersey in about two minutes suggesting about 30 minutes for the trip. (Try that in a car!). Since the rookery was destroyed by the building project the flight line has been discontinued but I've had reports of flocks of Rooks and Jackdaws now crossing the river in the direction of Aigburth. A project for Nature Watch listeners to follow up.

WILD GOOSE CHASE BECKONS: Shirley also told me that she'd seen geese – presumably Pinkfooted – flying inland in the morning and back towards Hightown in the evening. There didn't seem to be any suitable feeding grounds in the direction they were going , so a wild goose chase (literally!) would be another survey where NATURE WATCH listeners could help.

RUSH HOUR – ABOVE MERSEYSIDE: Not only Rooks and geese of course. At first light there are thousands of commuters criss-crossing in the skies over Merseyside! Gulls and Starlings move out from roosting areas. I have seen over 200 Magpies streaming out of a roost by Bidston Station. Herons are usually returning from night raids on park lakes – or your garden pond! Cormorants fly out to sea to their fishing grounds. No traffic jams, though it can get quite congested!

DIBBINSDALE – RABY: I've seen flocks of Rooks and Jackdaws circling over the trees in Dibbinsdale at dusk. They seem to arrive from the river and head off to roost in the direction of Raby.
Eamon Farrell

9 NOVEMBER: PIER HEAD TO PARADISE (STREET) NATURE TRAIL: Bitter cold north wind but beautiful sunshine, almost warm in sheltered spots. First snow in Scotland and north of England. 15-20 Goldfinches now feeding on the alders in Chavasse Park where the Yellow Balsam was still in full flower. Mistle Thrush on cotoneaster. Three Cormorants on the small landing stage at Canning Dock. Grey Wagtail on the quayside.

WOODCOCK IN NETHERTON: When we were in Dibbinsdale last Sunday you were talking about Woodcock. I've just seen one – flying over the police station in Copy Lane!
John Clegg

URBAN FOXES:

WHEELIE BIN PROBLEM IN AIGBURTH: Since wheelie bins were introduced recently in Aigburth the foxes (and the rats!) I used to see seemed to have disappeared. They obviously can't just knock off the lids like they could with the old bins.
Justin Garside-Taylor

SLY FOX AT ANGLICAN CATHEDRAL: One of our security men told me that he had seen a fox carrying off the 'ginger' rabbit which had become a favourite here with many visitors and staff.
Maurice Bray

BIG RESPONSE TO NOVEMBER FLOWER SURVEY: From listeners' reports I was able to put together a list of just on 70 (!) different wild flowers still out or showing some colour compared with 15-20 offered in the books for a normal November. The same in gardens:

WAVERTREE: The forsythia next door is starting to show yellow flowers again, brightening the trellis between our houses.
Margaret Thompson

AINTREE: Altogether – garden flowers, wild flowers and 'weeds'- I've counted 47 different kinds of flower still showing colour.
Mrs F. Heyes

WARRINGTON: I heard you talking about the mild weather and its effect on our gardens and plants. I counted 26 different kinds – and a dandelion! I also picked the last runner beans and courgettes yesterday and still have spinach to pick.   Dilys Williams

SUNDAY 11 NOV: POPPY DAY: REMEMBRANCE SUNDAY IN GARSTON
Nature Watch: the next generation

We passed the Cenotaph in Long Lane on our way round and down "Under the Bridge" with Sally and Alan Jones as our guides. Hidden wonders and treasures everywhere. A vineyard in Garston? Yes! In St Michael's churchyard we saw the grave (with dying swan motif) of the Portuguese family who planted them – hence Vineyard Street. The Dock Hill should clearly be kept as a local nature reserve like the old gasworks site on Banks Road:

"The old site of Garston gasworks is one of the most interesting and certainly the most natural area of land in South Liverpool. I have so far recorded 44 species of shrub, 21 grasses, 17 rushes and sedges, 82 wild flowers, 7 ferns, 31 mosses and liverworts, 32 species of birds and 16 species of butterflies."

Stephen Fletcher in the Garston News

Down on the Mersey shore the group was surprised to find themselves at the old Speke airport. Waders, Herons, a Red Breasted Merganser. Barn Owls have been seen hunting here and foxes have been getting fed at the Victoria in King Street.

14 NOVEMBER: WEST KIRBY'S SLEEPING BEAUTIES: I went to see Irene and Edmund Jelley who had invited me to see the butterflies which always hibernate in their top floor rooms. Five behind the wardrobe, three under the bed, one under the bed-side table, a cluster of five in a corner up by the ceiling. The same again in another room – altogether we found at least 35 Small Tortoiseshells and one beautiful Peacock still quite active.

16 NOVEMBER: CHILDREN IN NEED SPONSORED BIRDWATCH: Robin, Blackbird, Mistle Thrush (singing loud and clear from the law courts), four species of gulls, Pied Wagtail, a total of at least 60 Cormorants flying out to the mouth of the river, an unexpected Rock Pipit on the tidal steps at Kings Dock, pigeons, of course, Magpie. Starlings arrived as it got light and enjoyed a picnic with the gulls from the waste bins in Kings Dock car park. Seven Redshank and a fairly tame Heron on the beach, Wren singing, Hedge Sparrow and Greenfinch calls. Grey Wagtail over and my favourite Goldfinches were in Chavasse Park as I returned to the studio from the PIER HEAD TO PARADISE (STREET) NATURE TRAIL. 20 species of birds at 10p per bird makes £2.00. I asked listeners to add those two pounds to the pledge they were going to make during BBC TV's evening Children in Need spectacular.

16 NOVEMBER: NATURE WATCH NEWS

There was a fantastic response to our November flower survey. In all just on 70 different wild flowers have been found showing at least some colour still, whereas the books only offer 15 – maybe 20 for a normal November. Similarly in gardens: one garden still had 47 varieties (shouldn't that be 57?!). Red Admiral butterflies seen on 4, 9 and 13 November. On 14 November I went to see a house in West Kirby full of hibernating Small Tortoiseshells – and one Peacock. We found at least 35 – behind wardrobes, under beds etc, so check yourselves! A Crow was seen playing with twigs – thinking of nest building already?!

But the weather did change. On 8 November first snow in Scotland and north of England . On 13 Nov I saw the snow on the Welsh mountains for the first time this winter, but here, down around the Mersey itself, it is likely to stay quite mild. In fact Woodpigeons and Fieldfares have been moving east, probably to avoid frostier weather in Wales and heading for the milder prairies of South Lancs where most of the Icelandic Pinkfooted Geese and Whooper Swans have now arrived for the winter. The geese are also seen regularly over Netherton and Ormskirk so watch out for them e.g. from the train between Hall Rd and Hightown.

Bitterns have also turned up – at Wigan Flashes and two at Moore by the Mersey between Runcorn and Warrington – almost certainly winter visitors from Europe rather than wandering British Bitterns from Leighton Moss etc.

Salmon have been confirmed coming back into the Mersey – cleaner now than at an time in the last 200 years! Also regular sightings of Grey Seals in the river.

Any truly city-centre foxes? Late night revellers please report! The nearest report we have so far is at the Anglican Cathedral where sadly the tame 'ginger' rabbit which had become a favourite with visitors and staff was one of its victims – seen being carried off by the fox by security.

No more sightings of the Ravens at the cathedral (since 13 Sept) but one was over St Hilary's church, Wallasey on 13 Nov – another potential nesting site. Also news of yet another pair of Peregrines – still to be confirmed – in Birkenhead dockland which make four pairs within a couple of miles of the Pier Head! One still around Woodside at the beginning of the month.

I am just in the process of defining the area on both sides of the river which could be/ should be designated the Mersey Metropolitan (National) Wildlife Park. eg Seaforth to Garston; New Brighton to Eastham with a mile or two of hinterland. That will include all the waders and woodland birds you want! Barn Owls nesting within that area raised three young this year. A Canada Goose in Central Park, Wallasey, was ringed near York in 1992 and used to go up to Inverness for the summer before deciding to become a resident Merseysider! Swans in Newsham Park from Warrington and Chester. Beautiful sunsets at this time of the year – and sunrises when I walk the Pier Head to Paradise (Street) Nature Trail!

SUNDAY 18 NOVEMBER: THE WHABBS – RIMROSE VALLEY

Over the footbridge from Seaforth Station, turn right and into the 'new' country park. A beautiful Grey Wagtail was waiting for us on the path, Goldfinches in the trees. Through the 'swamp' to the football field where noisy Common Gulls were chasing Blackheadeds. Out onto the top of the 'moor'. A Sparrowhawk chased by a Crow, then off again gliding, flapping on another hunt. Starlings gathering on the pylon wires. 25 Lapwings flew south. Burrows by the canal looked like the work of Water Voles. Swans, Coot, Moorhen, Mallard – and an elusive little Dabchick which had us guessing where it would surface next. A wonderful male Pheasant playing ostrich, sitting tight out in the open, pretending we hadn't seen it. A friendly group of Long Tailed Tits. Evening Primrose in the Rimrose Valley, Fool's Parsley, Michaelmas Daisy, Hop Clover all still in flower. A 'typical' calm, grey November day – out in the wilds of Whabbs Common - alias the old tip! – between Crosby and Netherton…

CHRISTMAS SWITCH ON… and in time to be back at St George's Hall to see BBC Radio Merseyside's Tony Snell switch on the Christmas lights. On Friday at the Scouseology Awards (hosted by 'our' Linda) Tony had won the Radio Award alongside characters like Ricky Tomlinson and Claire Sweeney.

BEAUTY AND THE (LITTLE) BEASTS: When I was going home after seeing the fantastic Beauty and the Beast spectacular at the Empire I was fascinated to see a couple of mice playing along the underground railway track at Central Station – Wirral Line!   Margaret Eastman

THE FERNS OF CENTRAL STATION: Opposite the platform on the Northern Line a lot of rainwater leaks down the wall. This and the artificial light have made it possible for a whole colony of 'ferns and things' to thrive in subterranean surroundings.

SPARROWS AND SPARROWHAWKS: The overwhelming number of Sparrowhawk attacks witnessed in Merseyside gardens convinced me that they must be a major factor in the decline of sparrows. After all, they *are* called Sparrowhawks in this country! I can think of at least 20 just from memory. Formby, Mossley Hill, Stoneycroft, Netherley, Huyton, Gateacre, Garston on the Liverpool side; Spital, Thingwall, West Kirby, Bromborough, Wallasey Village on the Wirral side. Also sightings over the city centre, Chavasse Park, Albert Dock, Bootle Canal, Anglican Cathedral, Knotty Ash, Vale Park, New Brighton, Moreton, Liscard, Birkenhead Park etc. etc. etc. If we take just these 20 - at one sparrow per week - that makes 1000 sparrows a year. The reality is no doubt much more dramatic.

STONEYCROFT: The sparrow population has built up well in our garden – no doubt appreciative of the hedge for hiding from the pair of Magpies.

Fiona and Chris Marsden

Yes, the hedge will be vital to the sparrows. But for hiding from the Sparrowhawk rather than from Magpies.

Raven on south end of the Anglican Cathedral (Lady Chapel)

22 NOVEMBER: THE RAVENS RETURN:

Great news! I was in the cathedral workshop at about 9.00 when I heard a loud and familiar 'cruck, cruck' outside. I rushed out and looked up. Both Ravens were up on the cathedral at the nest site where they had nested last year.   Maurice Bray

More on the Ravens in the following Nature Watch News.

THE LIVERPOOL SQUIRREL...

BOWRING PARK: It was unusual to see a Grey Squirrel here, the first time I remember seeing one.   Frank Kingsbury

GARSTON: I've seen Grey Squirrels twice now in the park in Long Lane.

Kathy Andrews

FAZAKERLEY: Grey Squirrels have only just arrived in Bluebell Woods, posing a threat to the isolated population of Red Squirrels still hanging on here.

Paul Sutter

SEFTON PARK:I was surprised to see a Grey Squirrel in Sefton Park. I've never seen one here before. How did it get here? Did the city council introduce them?

Earl Kirkham

STANLEY PARK: It's only the last year or so that we've noticed Grey Squirrels coming into the park.   Jimmy McArthur

...AND THE WIRRAL SQUIRREL   (I've been dying to use that rhyme!)

Grey Squirrels were introduced to this country from America between 1876 and 1929 and have been spreading north from the Midlands. They have probably been in Birkenhead Park and Central Park, Wallasey for at least 20 years now. But they are only just becoming noticeable and regular in Liverpool city parks. The only explanation I can think of is that it would be easy for squirrels to get into the Wirral from the Midlands and Wales, but to reach Liverpool they would have to cross the Mersey via Widnes Bridge or at Warrington, so they have had to go the long way round.

SUNDAY 25 NOV: TREE PLANTING ON BIDSTON MOSS

Bidston Dock in 2000. By the end of 2001 most of the dock had been filled in.

National Tree Week. The tree planting was the ideal opportunity to see the upheaval that had been taking place around Bidston Dock. The restoration of the old rubbish tip was now more or less complete - thanks to the trees that we planted alongside Wirral's mayor John Cocker - in the pouring rain! Immediately adjacent to the site, Bidston Dock was being filled in with plans to extend the dockland sprawl right up to the foot of the new green hill. A waste transfer station was planned for the site of the defunct waste incinerator which should be demolished as a result.

We crossed Penny Bridge to view the dock site and to see the oldest house in Wallasey (1621), very much neglected and abused with industrial storage tanks right up to its doorstep, otherwise a once magnificent building. Outside a timber merchant's in Breck Road we found a fascinating variety of trees, obviously planted 'with loving care', including a Eucalyptus in full flower. Well it *was* summer in Australia! More destruction and loss of open space along Breck Road (see report on 28 Sept) but the day finished on a brighter note - a beautiful male Shoveler on the pools at Bidston Station, the first time I'd ever seen one there.

27 NOV: NATURE WATCH MEETS ORMSKIRK 'KES': Thelma had sent me a list of regular feeding times when 'Kes' turned up for the liver she put out for her. I went out to see for myself and sure enough, right on schedule, Kes turned up, gulped down as much liver as she could and then picked up the last piece, hopped up into the rockery and stowed it away for later. Already ten years old, long may she reign!

30 NOV: PIER HEAD TO PARADISE (STREET) NATURE TRAIL: Andy Ball reminded me that it was St Andrew's Day and challenged me to find something Scottish on my way round our city centre nature trail. I managed to track down a haggis (cornered in St John's market) but when I got back to the studio at 8.00am...GEORGE HARRISON IS DEAD: The news came as no great surprise to most people as it was known that George had been suffering from throat cancer. Nevertheless the worldwide reaction to the news was probably much greater than expected. Flowers in Mathew Street, books of condolence, a day of grief.

30 NOVEMBER:NATURE WATCH NEWS

Just when I was expecting to report that everything was settling nicely into a winter routine great news came in. The Ravens had been seen back at the Anglican Cathedral. A reminder of the story so far:

Ravens first nested on Chester Cathedral six years ago - the first time Ravens had nested on buildings anywhere as far as we know. They usually nest on crags and cliffs, also in tall trees in some places. In 1999 a pair turned up on the Anglican Cathedral in Liverpool, built a nest, but didn't lay eggs. In 2000 they did and they were at the cathedral again early this year. But in March something must have happened which made the Ravens abandon the cathedral and any nesting plans. In June news came in of two other pairs of Ravens nesting on gasholders in St Helens and Southport. Then one Raven was seen around the Anglican Cathedral again on 13 Sept and now on 22 November the pair was back at the old nest site. They were there again next day at first light having clearly roosted the night there, so things look good for nesting next year - eggs usually laid in February and before that they still have to build a -very large - nest! Fingers crossed. (and there again on 2 Dec).

On 25 Nov I was told that a pair of Ravens had also nested in a tall tree in mid-Wirral this year and a pair of Ravens seen around Bidston Hill may well have been the 'missing' Ravens from the Anglican Cathedral. That evening Songs of Praise on BBC TV came from the Tower of London where we were introduced to their seven Ravens - wings clipped. We've got at least eight Ravens - all free flying voluntary residents!

Many people have commented on the wonderful display of autumn leaves this autumn but by the end of November the trees of Merseyside were starting to look bare at last. Even so, we are still waiting for the first real frost and many flowers have continued to show colour. Hedge Mustard - found on 'wasteland', car parks etc - should only be in flower in May-July according to the books, but there has been a complete second flowering which could become a regular occurrence if 'global warming' continues, especially in urban settings where artificial light, warmer temperatures and other factors such as 'fertilizer gases' (nitrogen) from car fumes create exceedingly favourable conditions for urban flora.

Mistle Thrushes and Song Thrushes have both been heard singing in the last two weeks - not unusual at this time of the year, though they too are encouraged by artificial light - singing best before daybreak! A Red Admiral was flying in Netherton on 13 November - and again on 30 November!

A Bidston Blackcap was recovered in Morocco, one of the main wintering grounds of British Blackcaps - which *do* migrate. Those that stay here for the winter have come from further north or east. Woodcock in Netherton and Central Park, Wallasey. A Snipe in Sefton Park(!). An escaped American Harris Hawk in Stanley Park. The family group of 9 Partridge still at Bidston Moss.

*Arnold Grove, 2 December
2002*

We agreed that the best way to pay our respects to George Harrison would be to go out to Arnold Grove where he was born and spent his early years. While we were there a solitary Grey Wagtail flew over. Then we crossed into Wavertree Playground - the 'Mystery' (the mystery being who had donated it to the people of Liverpool) A lot of House Sparrow noise along Prince Alfred Road - quite an unfamiliar sound in so many places these days. Common Gulls kept us amused, drumming with their feet to bring up worms. At least we were able to confirm that it does work! We ended the day with a Sunday roast back in the Grapes in Mathew Street where we saw photos of the Beatles there back in their heyday in the Sixties.

A WOODCOCK IN PARADISE STREET! Before we had set off for Wavertree I had come along Paradise Street to meet the Nature Watch team outside the BBC Radio Merseyside studios. I couldn't believe my eyes when I saw a dead Woodcock lying in one of the giant 'flower pots' by Custom House Lane. It had presumably been found dead on the pavement or in the road and somebody had put it there out of the way. Woodcock do turn up in some strange places in autumn and winter but this remained one of the most unusual finds of the whole year.

4 DEC: THE RETURN OF '7GB': In the first pages of this book I told how I had lost track of 'my' Mute Swans - male with blue ring 7GB and partner - back in September 2000 with no sightings since. As I was passing through Central Park, Wallasey, I saw a pair of swans - one with a blue ring, but I was sure it was asking too much to expect it to be 7GB. However, as it swam across in the hope of being fed I saw the number! 7GB was back. Where had they been for the last year or so? Had they nested successfully this year after disappointment in 2000? Apparently not, otherwise they would presumably still be accompanying young. They settled in at Central Park and stayed for the whole winter. Are they still there? Or where did they go?

Sefton Park, 9 December 2001

Having included the homes of George Harrison, John Lennon and Paul McCartney in our Sunday Nature Watch outings, it seemed only right to finish off with Ringo's. We started in Sefton Park where we found 60 Canada Geese on the lake. We warmed up in the Palm House and then the café before continuing to Princes Park where we saw the grave of Judy, the donkey who had been a favourite with local children and who died in 1926. Past Ringo's house in Madryn Street to the Empress pub - where we lost half the group! - whilst the others headed back into town for soup and a warm up.

A DECEMBER BUTTERFLY: Frank Benham told us he had been at Martin Mere the day before and a Small Tortoiseshell butterfly had flown past one of the hides!

10 DEC: BLUECOAT CHAMBERS: Merseyside Naturalists' Association Members' Evening:

The proceedings were opened by regular Nature Watcher Tony Whewell with a short presentation about the Killer Whale he had spotted at Woodside on 7 Oct, echoing the presentation made by T.J.Moore to the Liverpool Literary and Philosophical Society in April 1876 about the Killer Whale which had been beached at West Kirby - the only previous record for the region.

11 DEC: LIVERPOOL CATHEDRAL: BBC RADIO MERSEYSIDE CAROL CONCERT: In aid of the BBC Radio Merseyside Charitable Fund. Linda (McDermott) looked astonished to see me dashing past like a mad March hare round the back of the cathedral - to check if the Ravens were roosting there! What I did see was that the old nest site from 2000 remained dark even when the rest of the building was illuminated, presumably the reason why they had chosen that corner. Then inside for Hark the Herald Angels Sing!

14 DEC: PIER HEAD TO PARADISE (STREET) NATURE TRAIL: *And a Mistle Thrush sang in Derby Square* - substituting for the Nightingale of Berkeley Square fame! Grey Wagtail calls overhead confirmed they were still about. A single Redshank was down in Canning graving dock by the 'de Wadden' schooner - seen later on several more occasions, possibly injured in some way but able to fly well, it seemed.

GATEACRE GARDEN BIRDWATCH – BRITISH TRUST FOR ORNITHOLOGY

In March 1995, when I signed up with Garden BirdWatch (run by BTO) to record the weekly number of bird species visiting my garden, I little realised what a fascinating world I was about to enter. 6 ½ years and 29 species later I have a detailed record of the bird life of one small garden in South Liverpool. My figures confirm the dramatic decline of the humble House Sparrow from being the ever present top bird in 1995 to not appearing once in 1999! The good news is that it is on the increase again and this year will be recorded with over 40% presence. Although the Blue Tit is the most frequent bird over the entire period, the Greenfinch has now taken over as number 1. In May 2000, I hung some black sunflower seeds up and promptly recorded the first ever Greenfinch in the garden and it has been every week since!

One-off and occasional visitors are always exciting. Fieldfare, Siskin, Jackdaw, Song Thrush, Great Spotted Woodpecker and Sparrowhawk have each visited once, the last being recorded on the basis of a futile attempt to fly through the French window! Coal Tits came in the first three years, then a gap of two years and are now back again.

Continuous observation sees fascinating behaviours, like Magpies that learnt to dunk dried bread in the water dish before flying off with it.

There have been two exciting periods in 2001. In Jan / Feb the previous week record of 13 species was smashed with a 15 bird total (13 in one day!). Sparrow, Chaffinch, Blackcap and Goldfinch visited for several weeks, the Goldfinch being another first for the garden. More was to come in Nov/Dec when the record rose to 16 and there were three other weeks with 15. David Holland

WILDFOWL COUNT IN LIVERPOOL PARKS: In the winter of 2001/2002 David also took it upon himself to monitor the numbers of ducks, swans and geese on Liverpool park lakes with some very interesting results. For some reason Pochard favour Newsham Park where there is also a concentration of Mute Swans. In the frost in Jan 2002 over 200 Mallard came in onto Sefton Park lake. Tufted Duck in Calderstones, Teal in Princes Park and Sefton Park.

15 DEC: THE MERSEY MARSHES, STANLOW POINT: The Dee marshes, yes, but many people probably don't even know that there is a similar vast area of marshland on the Mersey estuary itself – along the Manchester Ship Canal from Ellesmere Port to Frodsham and the Weaver Estuary, where Little Egrets nested for the first time in 2001. The birds on the Mersey and Dee are very much the same but on the Mersey access is difficult – at present only by special permit via Stanlow Oil Refinery. It would be nice to think that in future access would be possible from the Boat Museum in Ellesmere Port especially as it is here just across the Manchester Ship Canal that myriad numbers of waders feed. On the other side of Stanlow Point large numbers of Teal were feeding along the mouth of the River Gowy and on the marshes in the distance we could make out several hundred Canada Geese. A closer inspection also revealed 4 Whooper Swans, a Bewick and a single Brent Goose. All this with the Anglican Cathedral and Liverpool skyline in the misty distance.

15 DECEMBER: NATURE WATCH NEWS

Over the years somewhere between 300-400 species of birds have been seen in the wider Merseyside region. I have been able to put together a list – no doubt incomplete – of approximately 200 species recorded and reported in 2001. Just on 100 species of birds have been seen within three miles of the Pier Head which does not include the many visitors to Seaforth Nature Reserve - four miles from the Pier Head. 67 species were recorded within one mile of the Pier Head. At least 60 species nest within three miles; 36 within one mile and at least 14 species on the Pier Head to Paradise (Street) Nature Trail around Albert Dock and Chavasse Park.

Twenty-one species of butterflies were reported, 18 of them within 3 miles of the Pier Head, 11 within one mile (including Painted Lady) and nine on the Pier Head to Paradise (Street) Nature Trail.

Bee Orchids have only become established and widespread on Merseyside in the last 15-20 years. They have now penetrated right into the city centre, though the two most central sites in Leeds Street and Old Hall Street were both destroyed by developments towards the end of the year. Marsh Orchids are also abundant – thirty in Paradise Street-Canning Place itself! Buddleia, Hemp Agrimony, Purple Toadflax, Hedge Mustard are amongst the characteristic flowers of city centre car parks and 'wasteland', with others such as Melilot and Teasel starting to appear. Wild or Yellow Balsam, a very local species, grows on the edge of Chavasse Park.

The highlight of 2001 was, of course, the Killer Whale spotted by the Nature Watch Team off Woodside on 7 Oct, the only other record for the region being one stranded at West Kirby in 1876.

Three, possibly four, pairs of Peregrines nest within 4 miles of the Pier Head, two of them just a mile away and visible from the Pier Head if you know where to look! At least four pairs of Ravens are nesting on Merseyside. The pair which nested on the Anglican Cathedral in 2000 returned in Nov-Dec, raising hopes that they would nest again in 2002. Buzzards, increasingly dramatically in Cheshire, now nest within 8 miles of the Pier Head with regular sightings over all parts of Merseyside. At least six pairs of Barn Owls nest on the perimeter of built-up Merseyside, which compares very positively with 15-20 pairs for the whole of rural Cheshire. Many Grey Wagtails nest in urban and dockland areas where artificial light and heat provide a suitable microclimate and habitat. Little Egrets nested for the first time ever – at Frodsham, 13 miles from the Pier Head.

There was a record spring passage of Little Gulls on the Mersey with over 800 at Seaforth. A record 172 pairs of Common Terns nested at Seaforth, only four miles from the Pier Head. September gales brought Leach's Petrels, Black Terns and other seabirds to the Mersey off the Pier Head.

A poor year for migrant butterflies after the big influx of 2000, but the mild autumn meant many late butterflies: Red Admiral until 30 Nov; Small Tortoiseshell until 8 December! Similarly flowers: about 70 species were still showing colour in November (compared with about 20 offered by the books), 45 into December.

SUNDAY 16 DEC: FERRY CROSS THE MERSEY

Liverpool or Venice? Glorious winter sun on our way to Woodside

As a Christmas finale the plan was to do a 'lap of honour' on the ferry, stopping off at both Seacombe and Woodside. The Redshank which I had seen in Canning graving dock on the Friday was there again as we walked down to the Pier Head. At Seacombe we walked up to Briardale Road where the story of 2001 had started with Waxwings on the rowan berries there. No Waxwings this winter, but the local Mistle Thrushes were still around, guarding their winter larder. At Woodside we staged a reconstruction of 7 Oct when we had seen the Killer Whale as we walked along to Monks Ferry. No Killer Whales this time so we installed ourselves in the restaurant for a Scouse Christmas Dinner. Most of those attending had responded to my request to wear something red, so if you saw a group of 'red robins' at Woodside Ferry that day you know what was going on! I then presented the Nature Watch Awards – certificates to those who had been regular Nature Watchers or who deserved recognition for some other reason. We did find time to have a look a Morpeth dock gates where we were surprised to find a Pintail. Over to Pacific Road where there was a Victorian Christmas Fayre, a lovely atmosphere to finish off with. And to cap it all, as night fell, an illuminated procession came by, wishing 'Happy Christmas to One and All'

21 DEC: PIER HEAD TO PARADISE (STREET) NATURE TRAIL:It was very bright and blustery, but exceptionally mild when I went out to have a last look around our city centre 'nature reserve', looking for old nests now that the trees were bare. During the course of the winter we found at least ten old Goldfinch nests: two on the Pier Head itself with another two in the trees along Mann Island, one between Canning and Salthouse Dock which I had walked past many times during the summer without realising! And as well as the nest by the Yellow Submarine, there was one right on Derby Square. Yellow Melilot was still in full flower down by the Super Lambanana on Wapping, Red Clover, Nipplewort and Sowthistle on the edge of the Moathouse garden. A Grey Wagtail was still about, the one bird which had thwarted my attempts to find its nesting site, probably down by the Baltic Fleet. Next year perhaps. In fact, for me, the new year was already starting: 21 DEC Winter Solstice, when the days would already be growing longer again.

21 DEC: NATURE WATCH NEWS

MERSEYSIDE: A MARITIME AND URBAN WILDLIFE NATIONAL PARK?

At our Christmas finale at Woodside Ferry the Nature Watch Team signed a 'unilateral declaration' that :

> *'We recognise the existence of the Merseyside Maritime and Urban Wildlife National Park.'*

It was on 16 March that I had first written that we wanted to turn Merseyside into the biggest wildlife park, the biggest 'nature reserve' in the country. By the end of 2001 we were satisfied that we had done it. There is nowhere else that can offer such a variety of wildlife in the very heart of a built up area as Merseyside can.

All landscapes in Britain are essentially manmade, whether they be rural-agricultural or urban-industrial. Birds and other forms of wildlife exploit all these landscapes and today urban and dockland habitats are of ever increasing importance.

The 'National Park' is already there, whether it has official recognition or not. All we have to do now is to observe and record the rich and varied wildlife present.

Dear Bob,   *1st January 2002*

I am writing to thank you for our Sunday Nature Watch walks. There have been some wonderful, interesting and at times some very funny moments. I can remember lots of special occasions, such as the Little Grebe on the canal, the gull stamping its feet trying to dance out the worms and the wonderful fall of golden leaves in Dibbinsdale…

It only leaves me to say thank you once again for a very enjoyable year.

Margaret Eastman

I have included this extract from Margaret's letter because it shows how the weekend Sunday Nature Watches did indeed add up to make it feel as though we'd been on holiday all year long (even though Margaret and many others were doing a full time job during the week). It was one continuous exploration of the fascinating planet we live on. I for one certainly didn't feel the need to go any further afield to enjoy the natural world around us. It's all here right on our very doorstep!

Bob 'The Birdman' Hughes

NOTES

THESE PAGES ARE FOR YOU TO MAKE ANY ADDITIONAL NOTES OF YOUR OWN, WHICH MAY FEATURE IN FUTURE *BBC RADIO MERSEYSIDE* NATURE WATCH PROGRAMMES AND BOOKS

FORGOTTEN EMPRESS - The Tragedy of the Empress of Ireland - by David Zeni

'...dubbed 'The 'Forgotten Empress'...the second in a shocking trio of tragedies at sea...sandwiched in between the disasters of the Titanic *and the* Lusitania, *...it was a sudden death... that sent Liverpool into mourning...'* Liverpool Echo

ISBN 1 902964 15 2   £12.50 inc. p&p

LUSITANIA   by Colin Simpson

More than eighty years on the story of the Lusitania continues to be shrouded in mystery and suspicion. What was her real cargo? Why wasn't she protected? Why did she sink so quickly? The Facts, the fictions, but most of all..the truth.

'A book that clamours to be read...' - The Observer

ISBN 0 9521020 6 4   £11.00 inc. p&p

LUSITANIA AND BEYOND - the Life of Captain William Thomas Turner
by Mitch Peeke and Kevin Walsh Johnson

Over the years Captain Turner has been accused of treachery, stubbornness, ignorance and much worse. This book gives the true, remarkable story of Captain William Thomas Turner, the last Master of the doomed *Lusitania.*   ISBN 1 902964 14 4   £9.50 inc. p&p

LIFE AT LAIRDS - Memories of working shipyard men by David Roberts

"When Cammell Lairds has gone and we are a generation or two down the line who will answer the questions 'What did they do there?' 'What was it like?' This book answers the questions." - Sea Breezes

'A Piece of Social History'   - Liverpool Echo

ISBN 0 9521020 1 3   £ 8.00 inc. p&p

{**CAMMELL LAIRD - Old ships and Hardships:** on Video. £14.99 inc. p&p in UK}

CAMMELL LAIRD - the golden years by David Roberts.

'Captures life in the prosperous years of the historic Birkenhead shipyard'
- Liverpool Echo

'*Puts into perspective...the strikes...the Polaris contract...and those who worked at the yard*'   - Sea Breezes

ISBN 0 9521020 2 1   £7.60 inc. p&p

UNION - CASTLE - The Forgotten Navy by Peter Abbott

Features the Intermediate liners, The Royal East Africa Service, Round Africa vessels, coasters, general cargo ships and reefers. Also covers the Zulu War, Boer War, World War I and World War II.   ISBN 1 902964 21 7   £11.00 inc. p&p

IRON CLIPPER '*TAYLEUR*' – the White Star Line's 'First Titanic' by H.F. Starkey

'Iron Clipper' is subtitled 'The First Titanic' for it tells the story of the first White Star liner to be lost on her maiden voyage. The '*Tayleur*' tragedy of 1854 and the '*Titanic*' catastrophe of 1912 are disasters which have so much in common that the many coincidences make this book appear to be a work which is stranger than fiction.

ISBN 1 902964 00 4   £8.00 inc. p&p

CLAN LINE IN PHOTOGRAPHS - VOLUME ONE
- THE FIRST 40 YEARS: 1878 - 1918. by Tony Blackler

Clan Line Steamers Ltd. was perhaps typical of the British merchant cargo fleet until the arrival of the container. As far as we know there has been no definitive history written about the whole company, generally known throughout the last century as Cayzer Irvine & Co. Ltd. This first volume of old photographs compiled from the collections of Bob Briscoe and the author (both ex-company employees) will certainly go some way to revive old memories.

ISBN 1 902964 3 3 0   £9.50 inc. p&p

A WELCOME IN THE HILLSIDES ? by Jill Wallis
The Merseyside and North Wales Experience of Evacuation 1939 - 1945

A book that is both informative and moving, with the real-life stories of the thousands of children who left the dangers of Merseyside for the safety of North Wales during World War II.

ISBN 1 902964 13 6   £12.00 inc. p&p

JUST NUISANCE AB - His full story by Terence Sisson

The amazing but true story of the only dog that was officially enlisted into British Royal Navy, a Great Dane whose name was Nuisance, his official rank and name was AB Just Nuisance. Famed for his preference for the company of navy ratings (he wasn't too keen on Officers) in and around the famous World War II naval base of Simonstown, South Africa, Nuisance helped many a sailor rejoin his ship after a night on the town.   £8.00 inc. p&p

FROM BATTLEFIELD TO BLIGHTY by Arthur R Smith
A History of Frodsham Auxiliary Hospital 1915-1919

The horrors of the first 'Great War' are well known, but the stories of those sent back from the *Battlefield to Blighty* tend to be overlooked. This is the little known story in words and photographs of one of the largest auxiliary military hospitals in the country that was established at Frodsham in Cheshire during World War One.

ISBN 1 9029640 16 0   £8.60 inc. p&p

FASTER THAN THE WIND - A History Guide to the Liverpool to Holyhead Telegraph.
by Frank Large

The coastline of North Wales and Wirral is spectacular and on a clear day it is possible to see just how signals and messages about shipping were sent along the coast to and from Liverpool. This book contains full details of the intriguing and little known sites of the substantial remains of the Liverpool to Holyhead Telegraph Stations.

ISBN 0 9521020 9 9   £10.00 inc. p&p

TO ORDER BOOKS OR VIDEOS DIRECT CONTACT:-

Avid Publications, Garth Boulevard, Hr. Bebington, Wirral, Merseyside UK. CH63 5LS.

Tel / Fax 0151 645 2047

Look at the books and videos via the internet on

http://www.avidpublications.co.uk or E-mail info@AvidPublications.co.uk

Note. All prices here include postage and packaging within UK.